Development of an Environmental Bio-Industry:

European perceptions and prospects

EF/92/18/EN

ACKNOWLEDGEMENTS

It has been possible to carry out the present research project thanks to the kind attention and goodwill of a large number of correspondents and interviewees. The list of people who were contacted and people who were questioned is given in Annex I.

I would like to thank all those who allowed this study to go forward, as well as thanking the European Foundation in Dublin, especially Mr C. Purkiss and Mr R. Anderson, for entrusting me with the task of writing this report. My thanks are also due to Ms Eirlys Roberts (ERICA, London), who chaired the Dublin seminar, and Ms Camilla Galli da Bino of the Foundation, who looked after its practical organisation.

European Foundation
for the Improvement of
Living and Working Conditions

Development of an Environmental Bio-Industry:

European perceptions and prospects

by
Anne-Marie Prieels
TECH-KNOW
Brussels

Loughlinstown House, Shankill, Co. Dublin, Ireland
Tel: +353 1 282 6888   Fax: +353 1 282 5456
Telex: 30726 EURF EI

Cataloguing data can be found at the end of this publication

Luxembourg: Office for Official Publications of the European Communities, 1993

ISBN 92-826-4691-2

© European Foundation for the Improvement of Living and Working Conditions, 1993

For rights of translation or reproduction, applications should be made to the Director, European Foundation for the Improvement of Living and Working Conditions, Loughlinstown House, Shankill, Co. Dublin, Ireland.

Printed in Ireland

"It is through processes of interpretation that we cognitively construct actual or possible worlds."

UMBERTO ECO,
The Limits of Interpretation, 1990

PREFACE

The Foundation's work on biotechnology has been developed to support dialogue and debate on this key field of development. The first phase of this work involved studies of the implications of applications of biotechnology for living and working conditions. One of these reports considered the impact of biotechnology on the environment, including the potential value of biotechnological processes in environmental management (see Annex for abstracts of earlier Foundation publications). In subsequent work on scenarios for the development of biotechnology in Europe (Yoxen and Green, 1990), the authors emphasise the importance of public concerns about the environment as a factor influencing the future of the technology.

The current report makes a distinctive contribution to the Foundation's recent work, organised under the umbrella theme of 'attitudes to biotechnology'. It tackles the complex but essential problem of trust and confidence in communications about biotechnology. Through a literature review, a series of interviews and a workshop, the author develops her ideas about the necessary conditions for meaningful dialogue on the application of biotechnology for pollution control and improvement of the environment. The prospects for applying biotechnology for the environment are shown to be bound up with technical, economic and regulatory conditions, but also ubiquitously with the quality and transparency of interactions between industry, public interest groups and government.

This synthesis of developments and perspectives is intended to support identification and discussion of the sensitive issues involved. As the author's preface acknowledges the complexities are reflected in the arguments and dilemmas presented in the text. The report is designed to offer a variety of perspectives, although the author's training as a scientist is apparent. The conclusions and specific recommendations are important for the wide range of key players - in government, business, trade unions, media, public interest groups and science - who are influencing prospects for the beneficial application of biotechnological processes. Underlying a note of cautious optimism is an awareness of the urgent need to improve communications between science, industry and the public.

AUTHOR'S PREFACE

This report comes within the framework of the programme of work of the European Foundation Dublin, concerned with "public attitudes to biotechnology".

It follows up the reports by M. Kvistgaard and A. Meulengracht: "Impact of biotechnology on the environment - a literature review of environmental applications and impact of biotechnology", carried out for the Foundation in 1987.

The aim of the present report is to contribute to the answering of two questions:

1. **Is biotechnology capable of contributing to an improvement in the state of the environment, and more particularly, can it be utilised to improve the performance of procedures for treating pollution and nuisance factors?**

2. **Why is this bio-industrial sector not more highly developed in Europe?**

It was clearly necessary to survey the present position on the **prospects** offered to the European environmental bio-industry.

The answers to these questions were to be worked out on the basis of observations bringing together the information assembled by consulting the literature, on the one hand, and meeting experts from all the areas involved, on the other hand. These sources also provided **points of view** expressed by scientists on the one hand, and different groups of socio-economic and political actors on the other hand.

These points of view emerge from individual or collective syntheses between **factual** ("objective" or scientific) elements, elements of **interest** (economic or political), of **value** (ethical, spiritual) or of **ideology**.

The polemical and contentious nature of the ongoing debate on the utilisation of the latest achievements of advanced technologies poses the problem of information sources. In fact, it is still difficult even today, in this area, to refer to sources which are not immediately impugned by one or other interest group. I have therefore been careful to cite my sources, thus giving the reader an opportunity to reach a personal opinion on their quality.

In the same spirit of openness, whenever I have had to put forward a personal opinion, I have indicated clearly that this was the case.

This study was initiated at a time when the debate on biotechnology (more particularly genetic engineering) in Europe was taking on its full significance: decisions were about to be taken, especially under the form of directives designed to control the use of genetically manipulated organisms in the environment.

In all areas concerned with environmental questions, one difficulty never fails to emerge: how to operate a qualitative distinction between value judgements, conflicts of interest, and scientific objectivity.

These same difficulties may be observed in all debates concerned with different aspects of the development of genetic engineering (R. Straughan, in "Outlook on Agriculture," 1991).

The process of investigation and reflection for this research project thus quickly demonstrated the need to deal with the area of **perceptions** as well as the area of **prospects**, as well as the problems of **communication** which lead to sharply divergent opinions between different groups - social, economic and political.

The political and regulatory framework in which bio-industry is set to develop conditions the environmental industry sector on two levels: the level of directives which **create the market** of the environment, and the level of directives which **control the utilisation** of genetic engineering.

This framework derives from the interpretation in political decision-making the public's perception of dangers connected with the introduction of new technologies.

The problems of communication which have been identified derive from - or lead to? - the lack of ability of institutions (particularly European institutions) to **integrate** considerations of a socio-economic and ecological nature into the regulations designed to control any possible risks associated with the use of genetic engineering, for example in the environment. And yet this integration is required, by the introduction of articles 130 R,S,T in the Single European Act.

(This general failure in the ability to integrate different aspects is also underlined by the United Nations Conference on Environment and Development, as something which renders institutions incapable of satisfactorily resolving the problems of the environment and development - cf. the Brundtland report).

The **compartmentalised**, sectoral type of decision-making which prevails at European level cannot fail, it seems to me, to lead to a greater **radicalisation** between those opposed to technological development and those supporting it. (It must be noted that the Commission has set up a Co-ordination Committee in the biotechnology area - but this happened after the promulgation of the recent directives controlling the use of genetic engineering.)

This study on the process of evaluation of change induced by the development of biotechnology is addressed to the research community, industrialists and European institutions, so as to raise their awareness of the need to achieve better communication of developments in knowledge and technology, but also of the conditions of our socio-economic development in all its aspects.

The conclusions and recommendations of this report are addressed essentially to the **European institutions,** with a view to demonstrating the desirability of more **dialogue and openness,** at all levels and in all decision-making sectors - as this dialogue is the only thing which can lead to greater integration, clarity and coherence in decision-making. This dialogue is often made difficult at the present time, given that certain representatives from political groups, interest groups or institutions refuse to take part in it (for example, it proved impossible to obtain statements of views from some of these people for the purposes of the present report).

On the other hand, it is necessary to secure an improvement of the ability of the public (the citizens) to handle (or digest) information concerning the **complex evolution** of our natural and socio-economic system, and the contradictory positions or even uncertainties expressed in relation to the different aspects of our mode of development. The disturbing success of simplifying and simplistic political arguments, in this area as in others, referring where necessary to various kinds of scapegoats, and refusing both dialogue and open debate, should serve to make political leaders aware of the threat which this represents for **democracies.**

One may wonder how legitimate is the hope of most scientists, in relation to the difficulties of securing acceptance of molecular biology, that the public might consider any advance in knowledge simply as **progress.** While everybody recognises - unless they are completely irresponsible - that it is necessary to ensure that new products are not harmful, and that development must maintain a degree of social equity (or even ethics), no alternative appears as valid as one which emerges from a **reasoned** use of our capacity to understand both our own nature and the nature of our environment. This cognitive adaptation to the unceasing changes in the universe, both human (if only in its demographic dimension) and natural, constitutes the only possible alternative if our species is to survive with dignity. The reasons why this point of view is not shared by public opinion - or by those who claim to represent public opinion - need to be taken on board as a matter of urgency; and the alternatives which could be proposed must be evaluated in all their consequences.

As indicated by recent documents from UNCED ("Environmentally sound applications of biotechnology"), genetic engineering is **neither "intrinsically dangerous nor intrinsically without danger"**. These same documents confirm that biotechnology can be used to **improve** the state of the environment. These are my own conclusions too. But the conditions for implementing these developments must be negotiated, so as to make it possible to attain their objectives in a manner acceptable to everybody, without compromising the possibilities of using the results of molecular biology, nor the possibilities of safeguarding the democratic feasibility of a **development largely based on science.**

This report constitutes a document "on science" and its development, not a scientific document in the strict sense, although many scientific references can be found in it. It represents an addition (or an alternative?) to the numerous documents published on the same subject by experts in the human sciences.

Anne-Marie Prieels

CONTENTS

I. Introduction 12

II. Conclusions of the study 15

III. Methodology 26

IV. Study carried out from September to December 1990 28

    1. The pollution treatment bio-industry 28

    2. The scientific and technological bases of the environmental bio-industry 42

    3. Acceptance of biotechnology. Influence of the development of applications in the environment sector 52

    4. Biotechnology and sustainable development 69

    5. The political and regulatory framework of the environmental bio-industry 73

V. Report on the seminar organised in Dublin (2-4 September 1991) 77

VI. Recommendations 101

Annexes:
    I. List of people contacted 108
    II. Bibliography 111
    III. Framework of analysis 118
    IV. Principal documents collected during the study 120
    V. List of participants invited to the seminar 122
    VI. List of communications presented by seminar participants 125

I. INTRODUCTION

The development of industrial applications of life science research findings has given rise to the activities of *"Bio-industry"*, which is appearing in many sectors of the economy with a transforming effect.

Biotechnology is used in particular by large companies in the chemical sector, human and animal health, and plant health. The products developed by these companies are capable of modifying the impact of certain economic activities on the environment. In recent years, a need to evaluate this impact has emerged, especially as regards the use of genetic engineering to improve micro-organisms, crops or animals. While most molecular biology experts believe that there are no objective risks of a new kind associated with these operations, certain ecology experts and certain pressure groups or political movements believe that the modification of organisms by recombinant DNA techniques introduces a particular kind of risk to the environment, and that it is therefore necessary to set up special regulations designed to control these risks. The interpretation of scientific data in this connection is not definitive, but political pressure has led European institutions, following the lead of some Member States (such as Denmark), to set up a system for monitoring operations for the production and use of organisms which have been genetically manipulated by recombinant DNA. In this area, the present report is concerned with evaluating the extent to which certain industrial strategies can favour the improvement of the environment, how they may be perceived by the public, or by opinion groups, and what improvements in the institutional context may favour these developments.

The environmental bio-industry properly so called, i.e. the **pollution treatment bio-industry** ("bio-treatments", "bio-reclamation", "bio-remediation") is a sector which in many ways presents widely varying characteristics. The companies involved are smaller in size than the chemical industries, and their markets are essentially determined by the severity of regulations relating to environmental protection.

The scientific expertise of this sector is based on microbial physiology and ecology and engineering techniques - molecular biology often lies outside the field.

For this sector, the analysis presented in this report consisted in evaluating the tendency for the companies involved to develop new applications, especially in genetic engineering, or the tendency for large companies, in the chemical sector for example, to enter these markets. An attempt has also been made to evaluate the perception of these applications of biotechnology by the institutions charged with protecting the environment, and with regulating genetic engineering operations - and the perception among opinion groups.

This analysis is thus centred on interactions between *bio-industry*, the *environment* and *society* - the latter being represented by political institutions, public authorities and opinion groups. The actual "public", on the one hand, and the market on the other hand (which will finally determine the future of current developments) are more difficult to identify, to understand and to represent: the public is seen as volatile, while the market is subject to confidential evaluation by the companies concerned.

Although some information can be obtained about the *perception* of biotechnology by certain groups of citizens in Europe, such information could not conceivably be thought to invalidate or validate those activities, or the regulatory measures adopted concerning them. Moreover, the interpretation of the data is open to debate, and any programme of measuring opinion runs the risk of causing reactions in one or other of the possible directions in which the debate may develop.

Similarly, it is difficult at the moment to evaluate the basis of scientific *knowledge* shared by a majority of Europeans, so that they can appreciate what is at stake in these debates at its actual value. Yet such a rational basis undoubtedly represents the only available ground for a negotiation of the conditions of our development based on science. Similarly, there is no mechanism for assessing the *information* given to the public, at the level of both content and semantics. Neither the scientific world, nor the industrial world, nor the political world seem to pay attention to the way in which unfounded rumours concerning science and technology can be spread: unfounded or badly presented information can give rise to unjustified fears or hopes, all the more difficult to handle because the public lacks specialist knowledge.

It has not been possible to deal with the relative effectiveness - in terms of communication or in terms of impact on socio-economic development - of the democratic processes of consulting the public, industrialists, and scientists, concerning the establishment of the current framework of regulations for the control of genetic engineering, in the United States and in Europe, but is clear that such an evaluation could lead to an improvement in the conditions for the development of bio-industry, and the perceptions of that industry, on both sides of the Atlantic.

II. CONCLUSIONS

II.1 EUROPEAN ENVIRONMENTAL BIO-INDUSTRY PROSPECTS

1.1 The European market for environmental industries is generally set to grow rapidly between now and the year 2000, when it could reach 100 billion ECU (cf. EC-DG III Panorama of European Industries, 1990). Experts using a "conservative" approach (cf. SAGB - ref. 28) estimate that less than 5% of that market is available to biotechnology-based pollution treatment methods, while others say it may reach 25% in the future (W. Verstraeten, Belgium). This optimistic scenario is justified by experts who assume that the concept of "bio"-degradability will be evolving, and that progress in areas like microbial physiology and ecology, on the one hand, and microbial genetic engineering, on the other hand, will lead to the development of microbes able to degrade currently undegradable substances.

Improvements in the competitivity of biological pollution treatment processes will depend on

- the actual growth of the "remediation" markets, which will be conditioned by the development of future environmental regulations (sanitation programmes, standards, economic instruments);

- future regulations concerning the use of micro-organisms (indigenous natural ones, exotic natural ones - and genetically modified organisms) in the environment, which will be conditioned by the state of scientific understanding and by the perception on the part of European societies of the actual risks involved;

- scientists and industrialists being able to solve a number of technical problems;

- polluting industries' awareness of the advantages and characteristics of biological processes, as opposed to chemical and physical pollution treatment processes. These biological processes do not cause, downstream, any emission of toxic pollution, unlike incineration, for example.

- the likelihood of the creation and growth of SMEs which often generate innovations but - unlike the multinationals - are often incapable of implementing the necessary strategies on their own.

1.2 With regard to the *environmental impact* of the applications of biotechnology, the situation is more varied, from the point of view both of science and of perceptions and public opinion. A real improvement in the way economic activities (industry and agriculture) impact on the environment will only be made possible through better *integration* of environmental objectives in economic decision-making processes (UNCED - Our Common Future, 1987), and through production processes being developed on the basis of an improved understanding of natural processes (i.e. life sciences research results). These are in fact the main findings of the Brundtlandt report. Bio-industrial processes are *in principle* coherent with such an integrative approach, since they *apply* life sciences findings. But at the present time there is no *objective* evaluation of the impact on the environment by industrial and agricultural activities, which compares traditional and biotechnological processes. Various **points of view** expressed about this issue are presented later in this report.

The author's personal conclusion regarding this is the following one: molecular biology provides means for improving the *cognitive* content of the various ways in which we are "manipulating" nature, and this might be one of the most important reasons for some people being opposed to genetic engineering. Such a novel approach in mankind's interfering with natural processes makes our responsibility and the mode of our relationship to nature more apparent, while simultaneously reducing the importance of chance in it. Some people are therefore not willing to allow humans the right to use what is perceived as a new power, either because it makes them look like gods, or because they do not trust scientists, industrialists or institutions. Nevertheless, a reduction like this (through increasing knowledge) in the significance of chance in our interventions in the evolution of natural processes, automatically reduces the role of uncertainties (and therefore of "dangers" or "risks").

II.2 CRITICISMS THAT HAVE BEEN EXPRESSED BY EXPERTS ABOUT BIOTECHNOLOGY AND ITS APPLICATIONS IN THE ENVIRONMENT

The criticisms and concerns expressed about the development of environmental applications of biotechnology can be classified as follows:

1) "Intrinsic" or "fundamentalist" criticisms: man should not change living organisms *by using molecular biology techniques* (such criticisms have not been expressed towards traditional breeding in agriculture). Man should not interfere with creation by using a *cognitive* approach (reference being made to the ethics that Nature prevails over man).

2) Specific criticism towards some industrial strategies, expressing concerns that socio-economic restructuring will affect social groups, and that such changes will be reinforced by the introduction of some of the biotechnological innovations (sugar substitutes, BST).

3) Specific criticism towards some industrial strategies which people think are leading to disruption of ecosystems (herbicide-resistant plants). (R. Goldberg - ref. 6)

4) Criticisms concerning the way R & D, production and distribution activities are currently implemented by academic laboratories, public institutions, small and large

companies, the regions of the world and the implications for the way in which access to information about the life sciences, natural resources, and the social and economic benefits of innovation will be distributed. These are essentially criticisms of the productivistic socio-economic development process.

5) Concern about the ability of scientists, national agencies (namely the ones which will be in charge of implementing European directives) and companies to control the risks of accidents. Furthermore, there are divergent opinions about the nature and probable occurrence of "accidents", and about the general character of "biological risk".

6) Concern resulting from the lack of sufficient understanding of environmental sciences in general, or of the ecology of r-DNA organisms. These are criticisms of our science-based development process.

7) Criticisms relating to the current communication and consultation procedures, and to the lack of "transparency", and to the level of knowledge of the issues insufficient to enable the decision-makers to form a sound opinion. These criticisms are rooted in some fundamental problems in the area under review:

- The difficulty in communicating between different - or even divergent - interest-groups, which have equally varied levels of scientific knowledge;
- The relative lack of transparency in the information processes set up by the research institutions and, even more importantly, by the industries involved;
- In certain cases, the public authorities mix up information and elementary instruction, while one may find industry presenting a mixture of objective information, marketing and advertising messages;

- The public authorities are sometimes accused of taking unbalanced decisions in favour of certain interest groups. This is another sign of a widespread loss of confidence in political decision-makers and, more particularly, in the mediating forces within the democratic system. Here again we are looking at a divergence between civil society and the actors of parliamentary democracy.

8) Finally, some representatives of the ecologist groups seem opposed to any attempt to solve environmental problems using "more science and technology". Rather, they would prefer a "global" approach in economic decisions, and the use of development processes which could reduce the need for pollution treatment.

Sometimes, all these criticisms are combined, and are expressed in relation to "biotechnology" in general, while actually referring to "genetic engineering" (or human reproduction medical technologies). There is confusion regarding the concepts as well as the aspects they deal with. They also seem to be stronger where there apparently is no provision for dialogue or concertation, where confidence is missing that institutions, politicians, industrialists and scientists are able to behave in a "humanistic" and "responsible" manner, or where they are rooted in ideological, philosophical or religious beliefs.

Perhaps the applications of the research results from molecular biology are "paying" in this way for the slowness (twenty years) of the economy in adapting itself to the new ecological awareness. On the other hand, the difficulty of comprehending a more mechanistic, unified view of the mysteries of life brought about by molecular biology undoubtedly makes genetic engineering harder to accept than the traditional techniques of breeding or hybridation, or other biotechnologies such as cellular fusions. Regulations have addressed themselves to the techniques of molecular biology, whereas chimerical monsters (such as the "geep") are impossible to conceive by modifying the genome gene by gene at molecular level. (Chimeras are, in fact, produced by cellular fusion techniques. The extreme complexity represented by the mixture of thousands of genes making up the heritage of two species is not - and will never be - accessible to molecular biology.)

A number of considerations relating to **communication** in this area are offered later in the present report.

The following should be noted:

1) Despite what has been said, in certain European countries such as France, Italy and Belgium, not only have appeals ("Téléthon", "Télévie") for funds to finance public research projects in molecular genetics received extensive support from the public, but they have not come up against any deep-seated opposition, probably because the nature of the research was emphasised less than the gravity of the health problems needing to be resolved.

2) The United Nations (UNCED) are organising the "Earth Summit" (Rio, June 1992), which includes an agenda item on "Environmentally Acceptable Biotechnology Applications". The documents from one of the preparatory meetings for this summit (New Delhi, October 1991), as well as the first available texts which will be presented at Rio, point to the essential positive aspects of biotechnology in the perspective of socio- economic development and environmental protection in the Third World.

II.3 CRITICISMS ABOUT THE CURRENT REGULATORY FRAMEWORK FOR THE CONTROL OF RISKS OF BIO-INDUSTRIAL ACTIVITIES

1) Some circles, especially among scientific researchers and industrialists, regard this framework as aiming at "controlling genetic engineering" rather than "controlling

risks of biotechnology processes and products". If this perception is correct, there is a danger that further fuel will be added to the feelings of fear relating to a hypothetical *intrinsic* danger linked to the use of genetic engineering.

2) The basic options chosen and the decision-making parameters used by the Commission's Environmental and Social Affairs directorates are different. In fact, DG V (Social Affairs) believes that criteria of pathogenicity are clearly established, and protection measures are laid down in cases of objective danger. DG XI considers that all organisms derived from genetic engineering represent an "intrinsic danger" and have to be subjected to administrative and monitoring measures. Moreover, the European approach is also seen as different from the one used by American agencies. The two contrasting points of departure are, on the one hand, an assessment of products and, on the other hand, an assessment of the processes whereby these products are obtained. Finally, the actual definition of a "biological risk" is not yet clear. The risks thought to be specifically associated with genetic engineering, compared to the ones associated with **other biological processes** (e.g. the use of pathogens in the manufacturing of "classical" vaccines), or **other ways of changing living organisms'** genes (e.g. traditional breeding in agriculture) or even **other ways of modifying agro-ecosystems** (e.g. introducing exotic organisms) have never been discussed.

(It should be noted that while this report was going to press, the American government published the bases for a probable change in its approach ("Federal Register" of 27/2/1992). This change would aim both at taking account of the economic cost of the measures imposed, and at deregulating wherever it can be demonstrated that risks are nonexistent.)

3) Apart from work safety rules, there is generally no regulatory framework for monitoring "biological" risks (i.e. traditional biological processes listed under 2), and thus it is impossible to make an assessment of the potential risks of genetic engineering, taking account of knowledge based on past experience.

4) The procedure which consists in allowing institutions and organisations to examine authorisation requests without any kind of validation procedure of the requests for additional information is seen by some people as jeopardising European industries' competitiveness. It is a lengthy procedure: information circulates from one Member State to another one, and there does not seem to be any limit to the number of requests for additional information which can be made by the national and European authorities. The examination procedure can thus be unduly prolonged by the intervention of a large number of different agencies. *This practice does not exist for any other class of products.*

5) Due to absence of objective ethical and socio-economic criteria in evaluation procedures, authorities could be tempted to use environmental or safety considerations to delay certain developments for ethical or economic reasons, by raising ecological queries - indeed, something similar has already happened in relation to patents or marketing licences.

6) Certain excuses given for adopting the current regulations refer to the need to calm people's fears, but in fact the singling out of molecular biology techniques and the imposition of such constraining control measures have placed legislators in an awkward position, to the extent that on the pretext of calming unjustified fears they may have preferred measures restraining technological change over actions designed to collect information and evaluate it objectively.

7) The relative lack of transparency in the process of preparing Community directives sometimes gives rise to fears about imbalance and bias which pressure-groups might inject into the process. These effects are seen as contradictory in documents which are prepared under the leadership of this or that Directorate-General. Some people perceive (or allege) an excessive influence wielded by the ecologists over DG XI, or by the industrial lobbies over DG XII.

8) The current notification system, required to monitor activities of genetic engineering, could be considered acceptable if it were intended to support the authorities in developing an objective knowledge base. This base would also facilitate a future *development* of regulations towards normalisation based on pre-established objective criteria, and an integration of the experimental base acquired in the definition of this legislation.

9) To compensate for the lack of concertation/integration of economic and environmental objectives, on the one hand, together with the political imperatives and scientific findings on the other, the Commission has set up a "Biotechnology Co-ordination Committee" - *but after these regulations had already been published*. This body falls under the General Secretariat, and should in principle (for all the parties concerned) improve the connection to the real world, and the acceptability, of European policies in this area.

Observations:

1) Industries need a clear and consistent framework within which to operate, and, for this reason at least, are not opposed to the existence of regulations.

2) The scope and limitations of the present study have compelled its author to focus on directives dealing directly with the environment and biotechnology; it is certain, however, that other legislative instruments will also have an important influence in the areas which concern us here, such as, for example, the texts proposed by DG III (the "novel foods" regulation) or DG VI (agriculture).

II.4 CONCLUSIONS

It is possible to get biotechnological (including genetic engineering) applications developed in order to improve the environment - but this will only happen if the **communication** process between science, industry and the public *improves*. Regarding this communication process, we may quote by way of conclusion from the recent report issued by the US National Research Council (NRC), entitled "Improving Risk Communication", which does *not* cover biological risks but is intended to provide guidelines for a *democratic* debate about technological risks:

> "It is mistaken, for example, to view journalists and the media always as significant, independent causes of problems in risk communication. Rather, the problem is often at the interface between science and journalism (...). Even though most people prefer simplicity to complexity, it is mistaken to expect the public to want simple, cut-and-dried answers as to what to do in every case. The public is not homogeneous. People differ in the degree to which they exercise control over exposure to hazards or remediation of undesirable consequences, the importance they attach to various consequences, and their tendency to be risk averse or risk seeking.

Governments and industry spend large amounts of money on research, and thus their concerns are usually well reflected in the information developed by that research. Individuals and citizen groups do not usually have the financial resources to fund research and thus do not enjoy this sort of access to information and influence over its generation. If a group of people that a risk communication is trying to reach feels that the system for generating information relied upon by that source does not consider the group's concerns, it may reject the information from that source as a basis for decisions about risks".

III. METHODOLOGY

III.1 REPORT OF RESULTS (CHAPTER IV)

Information was gathered on the basis of a bibliographical search, on the one hand, and discussions with a certain number of experts, on the other hand (see Annexes I and II).

The resources made available for this work (three man-months) did not allow original analyses to be undertaken, or statistical evaluations of the area in question to be produced. This contribution therefore consists in an attempt to synthesise and interpret the different points of view which were found, on the one hand, and recommendations for action to be undertaken by the European institutions, especially in the research field, on the other hand.

The framework of analysis used is represented by the questions which were put to the experts (see Annexe III).

III.2 SEMINAR (CHAPTER V)

The report of this process of enquiry and reflection was discussed and completed through a seminar, organised in Dublin by the Foundation, on 2, 3 and 4 September 1991. The proceedings of this seminar are reported in Chapter V. The discussions during the seminar were organised around five groups of key questions, which had been sent to the participants together with a preliminary version of the "report of results". Most participants at the seminar were drawn from among those who had been questioned as part of the original enquiry (cf. Annex V).

III.3 EVALUATION MEETING IN BRUSSELS (DECEMBER 1991)

Both reports (the initial report and the report of the Dublin seminar) were evaluated at a working meeting in Brussels. This evaluation led to a major reorganisation of the projects prior to this final report.

IV. REPORT OF THE STUDY

IV.1 THE POLLUTION TREATMENT BIO-INDUSTRY

a. EUROPEAN ENVIRONMENTAL MARKETS

Most studies of these markets envisage a **growth**, between now and the year 2000, driven in particular by pressure for improved environmental quality, and increased legal constraints regarding both prevention and reclamation.

While a major proportion of these markets will be expressed through public or industrial investments, purchases of services or products designed to make pollution treatment installations function, another less visible part of the market will be concerned with the improvement of industry's capacity to manage its waste products and its resources, especially by transforming current industrial procedures into **"clean (or cleaner) technologies"**.

The reader will find below some data cited by the available literature, concerning the European environmental markets. These data are concerned essentially with the **"visible"** portion of these markets.

EUROPEAN POLLUTION TREATMENT MARKETS - millions of ECUs (MUC) (1988, ECOTEC, U.K.)

	1988	2000
Water	10,500	15,000
Air	9,000	12,000
Waste	9,000	16,500
Remediation	1,500	4,500
Total	30,000	48,000

INDUSTRIES USING POLLUTION TREATMENT TECHNIQUES

(1988, ECOTEC, U.K.)

Energy	28%
Water	22%
Chemical	13%
Food	11%
Metallurgy	9%
Paper	6%
Cement	3%

EUROPEAN ACTIVITIES IN THE ENVIRONMENT SECTOR

(MUC) - (1990, Commission, DG III)

Air	Water	Waste	Noise	
1,400	12,700	14,600	200	Services
2,100	12,900	1,800	2,200	Equipment
500	9,800	2,500	2,500	Products
4,000	35,400	18,900	4,900	Total

General Total 63,200

EXPENDITURE OF THE EUROPEAN CHEMICAL INDUSTRY

(MUC) (1988, CEFIC)

Waste	1,205
Water	3,450
Air	1,980
Noise	148
Total	6,783

EUROPEAN ENVIRONMENT MARKET

(1989, SCIENCE AND TECHNOLOGY)

1987:   32,625 MUC   (of which Germany: 10,500)
2000:   52,500 MUC

Budget for Germany 1987: 8,625 MUC (500,000 jobs)
Reclamation cost: 150 million DM

CEC: PANORAMA OF EUROPEAN INDUSTRY (1990)

(1987) Environmental expenditure

	,000 MUC	EC %	% GNP	% population
EUR	39.8	100.0	100.0	100.0
B	1.2	3.0	3.1	3.0
DK	0.8	2.0	2.3	1.6
D	14.5	36.4	25.5	18.9
GR	0.2	0.5	1.1	3.1
E	1.2	3.0	7.2	12.0
F	7.7	19.3	19.9	17.2
IRL	0.2	0.5	0.7	1.1
I	4.6	11.6	17.5	17.7
L	0.0	0.0	0.1	0.1
NL	2.0	5.0	4.8	4.5
P	0.1	0.3	0.9	3.2
UK	6.8	17.1	17.0	17.6

PUBLIC/PRIVATE INVESTMENT - FRANCE

(1984, OECD)

Public: 822 MUC
Private: 85 MUC

% GNP EXPENDITURE ON ENVIRONMENT IN EUROPE

(1983, JOYCE)

B	1.0
F	0.8
DK	1.0
D	1.5
GR	0.5
IRL	0.5
I	1.0
L	1.0
NL	1.0
E	0.5
P	0.5
UK	1.5
EUR	1.25

The companies active in these markets are:

- companies supplying equipment and procedures for pollution treatment (water, air, waste, noise, etc.);

- service companies, capable of carrying out studies to analyse pollution problems and suggest technical responses;

- companies carrying out detailed reclamation operations;

- companies supplying products which make it possible for installations to function;

- lastly, certain companies (essentially in the chemical sector) which have satisfactorily resolved their own environmental problems, and now offer their expertise in this area to other companies (for example, the American Du Pont group).

In certain countries, studies on the reclamation of domestic pollution are carried out by specialist government agencies, which sometimes leads to distortions, as these same agencies are later charged with managing the installations which they have designed. Thus, they are obliged to live with their own design errors. This places these State enterprises in a position where in practice they cannot objectively evaluate any design errors and correct them in later programmes of action.

b.   **THE BIO-INDUSTRIAL POLLUTION TREATMENT MARKET**

The "biological" portion of the environmental market is currently valued at less than 5% of the total market:

WORLD MAKETS FOR BIO-TECHNOLOGY PRODUCTS IN THE YEAR 2000 (billions of ECUS) - (1990, CEFIC, SAGB)

	Health	Chemicals	Agriculture	Environment	Equipment	Total
Current market	1.2	0.1	2.4	0.4	1.0	5.1
Market in 2000	23.9	14.6	40.0	2.0	2.8	83.3

PERCENTAGE OF TOTAL MARKETS REPRESENTED BY BIOTECHNOLOGY PRODUCTS IN THE YEAR 2000

(1990, CEFIC, SAGB)

Instrumentation	50 %
Food	20 %
Health	18 %
Overall average	8 %
Chemicals	6.3%
Agriculture	3.3%
Environment	1.3%

On the basis of a total estimated environmental market in Europe of about 50 billion ECUs in the year 2000, the bio-industrial pollution treatment market can thus be valued at 1 billion ECUs. This amount essentially represents the expenses needed to implement biological reclamation procedures, **under the current meaning of the concept of "biodegradability", in ecological and economic terms.**

Biological treatments are not currently viable except for the reclamation of used urban water and certain kinds of industrial water, the treatment of agricultural effluents and wastes and, in certain cases, the treatment of household wastes, industrial wastes, soils, underground water or gaseous effluents. Companies specialising in "bio-treatment" or "bio-remediation" are developing in the United States and in Europe.

At the present time, the majority of biological procedures for the treatment of harmful substances are based on the use of natural micro-organisms, *"native"* or *"alien"* to the sites being treated. Certain industrial procedures (such as the bio-catalyser developed by the ARASIN company in Germany for the treatment of foundry effluent) are based on the use of enzymes.

Most of the experts questioned believe that there are prospects for further development in the biological reclamation sector, based on improved performance by the micro-organisms used, especially through the use of r-DNA genetic engineering. (W. Verstraeten - EFB - ref. 17 / CEED - ref. 18 / K. Devine - ref. 22 / S. Lindow - ref. 23 & 24)

The literature offers no "ecological" analysis of the possibilities offered by these prospects, compared to those offered by physical and chemical pollution treatment procedures. Such an approach should provide a comparative assessment of the alternative techniques which are available, both on a technical and financial level, and in terms of the quantities of materials and energy produced or consumed, or of the displacement of harmful substances. It is indeed possible that the biological character of the harmful waste treatment processes could make them more "acceptable" from an ecological point of view. In fact, these processes are generally based on a more "soft" and "natural" procedure, less massively industrial and in any case, producing fewer downstream polluting effects.

Some people in the pollution treatment industry believe that the users of treatment techniques for industrial pollution must be educated in this area. The engineers who have the responsibility of resolving environmental problems in companies within sectors which cause pollution tend to look for solutions inside their own areas of expertise: the chemical industry deals with its pollution by chemical procedures, the mechanical sector deals with them through incineration, etc. The biological and ecological "culture" of most engineers in the polluting sectors - even in the pollution treatment industry - remains inadequate.

Biological procedures for pollution treatment are perceived by the user sectors as more difficult to implement, because the polluting companies do not contain biological **"professions"**. Moreover, in the current state of technology, these procedures are often less flexible, and have difficulty in dealing with variations in pollution levels within effluents. It is also a more delicate matter to control them by automatic regulation systems, which have yet to be developed, and form the subject of R&D programmes within certain companies such as Lyonnaise des Eaux.

Some experts believe that R & D efforts in the pollution treatment sector have so far been essentially confined within the area of engineering science, rather than being set in a perspective of improved capacity to manage biological procedures in the strict sense, whereas only an improvement in the understanding of biological phenomena would make it possible for biological treatments to become more competitive.

The development of the biological environmental market will be determined by the considerations of a technical and economic nature mentioned above, but also by the development of priorities given to ecological problems, as well as the development of policies on economic development and environmental protection implemented at world level, at European level, and within Member States.

In this connection, the priority concerns at the moment are:

- management of surface water and underground water;
- climate change (greenhouse effect);
- atmospheric pollution (acid rain and ozone layer);
- deforestation (desertification);
- urban and industrial waste, as well as the reclamation of old dump sites;
- toxic wastes;
- agricultural pollution (nitrogen, phosphorous, pesticides)...

Biological treatment of harmful waste products offers the opportunity to resolve problems in most of these areas. (The use of biotechnology replacing other types of production process is also capable of cutting pollution from waste in various kinds of economic activity.)

The **"bio"-degradability** of municipal wastes is currently estimated at 65% - whereas 16% are "potentially" biodegradable, and 19% are non- biodegradable. The entire future of biotechnology in the pollution treatment sector is undoubtedly bound up with the 16% of waste products which are "potentially" biodegradable (W. Verstraeten, Belgium). The biological portion of the environmental market could thus reach 25% (which would represent a market of **12.5 billion ECUs**, in the most extreme hypothesis of a European environmental market worth 100 billion ECUs between now and the year 2000).

Conclusions: The biological proportion of the environmental markets in Europe is a major one, and could be expanded up to 25%, if the developments made possible through technological advances are allowed.

---

c. **RESEARCH AND DEVELOPMENT**

The different types of company involved in the sector are investing in R & D. We have found some information in the literature on this topic:

- SNITER (France)

    5.5% of the budget of companies in the Syndicat National des Industries du Traitement des Eaux Résiduaires (National Syndicate of Waste Water Treatment Industries) was spent on R & D (1989).

- O.T.A. (USA) - 1989

    Investment by American companies on R & D in biotechnology:

    1% of genetic engineering companies
    2% of major companies

    are devoted to these projects in the reclamation area.

- OECD (1989)

    R & D investments by American companies in biotechnology in the environmental and energy fields:

    $3.7 million (1984)
    $8.0 million (1987)

- Business Communications (USA, 1989):

    Research expenditure by American companies in the area of environmental biotechnology comes to 138 million dollars.

- Lyonnaise des Eaux (1989):

    The R & D budget for this company comes to 1% of the budget in the "water" sector. (This figure is different from the information given by SNITER: the divergence comes from a different definition of "R & D" activities.)

OVERVIEW OF THE EUROPEAN INDUSTRY (CEC, 1990)

Public R & D on the Environment

(thousands of MUC)

	1975 value	1975 % RD	1980 value	1980 % RD	1985 value	1985 % RD
DK	n.d.	n.d.	3.6	2.1	6.6	1.5
D	53.2	1.0	102.0	2.0	309.3	3.1
E	0.0	0.1	2.2	0.6	9.2	1.0
F	35.5	0.8	46.7	1.1	51.1	0.5
I	5.6	0.6	13.6	1.0	44.6	1.0
NL	n.d.	n.d.	n.d.	n.d.	53.7	4.1
UK	25.8	0.5	30.9	0.7	99.6	1.1
USA	190.2	0.9	171.7	0.8	259.5	0.5
J	50.8	1.5	60.3	1.6	n.d.	n.d.

European patents in the environmental area
Deposited by country of origin in 1986

	Total	Air	Water	Soil
D	309	139	110	60
F	62	7	25	30
GB	62	16	39	7
NL	23	2	18	3
DK	19	6	8	5
E	16	8	6	2
I	11	2	7	2
IRL	4	0	3	1
B	3	0	1	2
L	1	1	0	0
GR	0	0	0	0
P	0	0	0	0
EC Total	510	181	217	112
USA	257	79	107	71
J	109	44	38	27
Australia	40	12	11	17
CH	20	8	11	1
Rest of the World	115	28	59	28
Total	1,051	352	443	256

As regards R&D at European level, the pollution treatment sector has not been directly covered by European Community programmes on biotechnology. It is envisaged that a number of projects will be financed in this area in the framework of a section dedicated to pollution treatment technology within the European STEP programme. The environmental industry sector is not yet organised in a European federation. There is a "Eur Eau" organisation, covering the sector of drinking water, but a "Eur Eco" has yet to be set up.

Generally speaking, this sector remains essentially dominated by strategies of confining costs to an "acceptable" level @ which fluctuates wildly. Some studies expect environmental spending to grow from 1 to 3% of GNP in most Member States between now and the year 2000. The costs of controlling harmful substances are seen in any case as "too high", and the process of internalising these costs, currently taking place, will give rise to some restructuring of production and consumption functions. This sector is, in the opinion of most experts, very "traditional", and "prudent", and R & D is less prominent than in sectors with high added value. As regards public research in these areas, this is covered by certain programmes which have varied in size over the last ten years. At European level, the last Framework programme gave a much higher place to "environmental" research - especially in the area of pollution treatment techniques, clean technology and sustainable development.

But the introduction of new technology in this area, such as genetic engineering or approaches based on molecular biology, remains slower: the "craft" in this sector remains essentially based on the techniques of engineering (civil, chemical and mechanical) and indeed on microbial physiology and ecology. The scientific areas of pollution treatment are seen by most scientists as less "glorious" than the other sectors, and research in biological engineering (procedures for implementation, procedures for regulation and control, procedures for separation and purification) have not been covered by European Community programmes (E.J. Nyns, Belgium).

The coverage of these areas by R & D activities at European level, and better communication of their results, should theoretically lead to a better integration of ecological aspects of bio-industrial development, and thus an improved perception and even an overall acceptance of biotechnology.

But the encounter in economic terms between two multidisciplinary areas such as environmental science and biotechnology poses many problems of communication, of transfer of expertise, of training, and of individual motivation, which have not been resolved.

At the first symposium of **EERO** (European Environmental Research Organisation), dedicated to the topic of "Environmental Biotechnology" and organised by GBF (Braunschweig) in 1990, the following priorities were proposed for R & D in this sector:

1) Demonstration of the effectiveness and economic feasibility of "bioremediation" on a natural site;

2) Clarification of the complementary roles of natural and recombinant micro-organisms;

3) Checking that the organisms used do not produce toxic substances during the process of degradation of pollutant materials;

4) Broadening the number of chemical products which can be treated by biological procedures;

5) Studying the behaviour of new genotypes in the environment;

6) Developing methods for treating pollution by radioactivity and heavy metals;

7) Informing the public and the authorities about the costs and advantages arising from biotechnology in the pollution treatment sector.

IV.2 THE SCIENTIFIC AND TECHNOLOGICAL BASES OF THE ENVIRONMENTAL BIO-INDUSTRY

IV.2.1 THE ECOLOGY OF RECOMBINANT-DNA ORGANISMS

According to the Robert dictionary ecology is **"the study of the environments where living beings live, as well as the relationship between these beings and their environment"**.

A major proportion of current research in the ecological area is concerned with the identification of environmental hazards caused by the use of certain products or procedures.

Recombinant-DNA organisms are living beings (micro-organisms, plants, animals) whose DNA has been transformed by laboratory techniques which make it possible to target, at a molecular level, the nature of DNA sequences which are improved. These techniques are thus based on an approach which is different from traditional methods of improvement by selection and hybridation, during which gene pools are mixed by sexual pairing (in the case of vegetables and animals). Genetic codes for known and controlled characteristics can now be introduced, through recombinant-DNA "genetic engineering", in vegetable and animal species, and in micro-organisms.

The ecology of these organisms involves the observation of their behaviour in a natural environment, in the presence of populations of other organisms, "natural" and "recombinant". While ecology is a traditional science, the perception of its importance is new, and important progress remains to be made in the areas of the ecology of "traditional" cultivated species or "natural" micro- organisms of the soil, for example (National Research Council, USA, and the European STEP Programme). The scientific bases required for a comparative analysis of the ecological behaviour of **"traditional"** organisms (cultivated species) or **"natural"** (micro-organisms of the soil) and **recombinant-DNA** organisms draw on at least two different disciplines, and it is necessary to integrate the concepts and the findings of these disciplines: on the one hand, we have the ecology of species of organisms and the relevant environments, and on the other hand we have molecular genetics.

These two disciplines are as different as could be within the field of life sciences: the former is essentially descriptive, while the latter is deductive. The former has to account for the observed behaviour of organisms and populations, for exchanges of materials and energy within ecosystems, and for potential "dangers" which they represent for other species, while the latter approaches these organisms through the chemical components of their genes, the expression of the genes and their transmission from one generation to the next.

It is therefore essential that specialists in these two disciplines should come together so as to place themselves in a position to respond to questions which neither side had tried to answer. Society is putting those questions today to the users of genetic engineering: Do the organisms emerging from this technology represent a "danger" for the ecosystems into which they are introduced? How do they behave in relation to other types of organism? What are their predators and their preys? Are they persistent? Are the new genes which they contain transmissible to other organisms? How do they evolve?

The simplicity of these questions is quite unrelated to the complexity of the answers, or to the experimental procedures which might provide these answers. For most molecular biologists, it is unacceptable that these questions should be raised in relation to their activity, whereas they were never raised with the selective breeders who, for centuries, introduced "new" genes in agro-ecosystems. In the opinion of certain experts, the experience built up over thousands of years of development in "classical" agricultural practices represents a basis of available and appropriate information to anticipate and evaluate the effects of genetic modifications in the organisms being studied. It is even probable that some answers to the questions posed may be found among the findings of previous studies covering species and their environments: but the interdisciplinary **integration** of such research findings requires a certain level of competence, openness, willingness and motivation which was not to be found within either of the two disciplines. (The viewpoints on this question remain sharply divided, between those who hold that modifying organisms through r-DNA necessarily introduces a new type of hazard into the environment - which would justify the current European regulations - and those who maintain the opposite view.)

It must also be recognised that most of these questions were largely raised **before** the point where large-scale trials became necessary or possible, and the point when the economic advantages could be demonstrated for the corresponding products. These questions were also addressed to experts whose speciality did not match the subject of the questions (molecular biology could not provide answers in the field of ecology). On the other hand, some ecology specialists were little equipped to understand the **comparative** importance of genome modifications at molecular level for the functioning of ecosystems, **as compared with the effects of modifications through "traditional" techniques of improvement.** In short, the questions raised did not find answers because science had not posed them, judging them "inappropriate" or "without interest". And the **lack of answers** brought about reactions in public opinion, leading to the present situation.

On the other hand, and to a certain extent, problems of approaches based on **"corporate" loyalties** were found, dividing the specialists in molecular biology from their colleagues in traditional selection and ecology (E.J. Nyns, Belgium). A process which parallels this phenomenon can be observed in industrial and administrative settings (the chemical industry contrasted with traditional breeders, patents contrasted with plant breeders' rights).

Lastly, it must be recognised that some reactions of public opinion stemmed from concern about several linked problems: the acceptability of genetic engineering from an ethical point of view (in the area of human health especially), from the point of view of economic restructuring, of social problems connected with the development of "professional specialities", of safety in the workplace - and from the point of view of the possible effects on the environment. In this latter area, answers are always difficult to provide, since these questions are new and have not been asked in relation to traditional techniques - and science does not yet have appropriate methods to generate this type of response. Only objectivity, then, allows one to state that at the present time no accident has been produced and it has not been possible to identify any danger.

It was therefore to be expected that a certain **gap** would open up between the progress of research undertaken to develop genetic engineering, and research to evaluate the environmental effects of the introduction of the products of genetic engineering. The **disproportion between the fears engendered by inadequate public information and the objective risks connected with the use of genetic engineering, as well as the lack of preparation in the scientific and industrial world to deal with the questions which were being raised, have perhaps led the institutions to set up a regulatory framework which is too cumbersome,** and indeed inadequate.

The consequences of these decisions will be determined essentially by the measures for implementing the regulations, and the possibility of adapting the system which is put in place to the experience accumulated as it is put into action.

The European Community programmes of research in biotechnology (BEP/RAP/BRIDGE) included, from the outset, a section and some resources dedicated to the ecology of r-DNA organisms and the identification of the possible dangers connected with their use. The responses to successive calls for tenders in this area were not however judged satisfactory during the early years of these programmes. This reflected a lack of interest and competence among European scientists in these areas, and a lack of perception of the importance of these questions among the public.

The current phase of the BRIDGE programme involves a considerable number of projects designed to resolve these questions. It is **possible** that in a short time, the findings of some of these research projects may lead us to conclude that there is no objective risk **of a new kind** linked to the introduction of r-DNA organisms into the environment, or that these techniques involve risks of the same kind as those connected with the use of traditional selection techniques in agriculture. (We would not, however, go so far as others have gone, in stating that *pharmaceutical* products manufactured with the aid of r-DNA micro-organisms do not need to be controlled by methods other than traditional products. The challenge there is to adapt quality control to the development of manufacturing techniques based on bacterial production rather than on chemical synthesis.) It would be highly desirable that in the future the results of these researches should be taken into account when European directives are being formulated, or when current directives are being adapted.

Professor W. Verstraeten (University of Ghent) observes: "To make a genetically modified micro-organism capable of surviving in the environment - outside the laboratory - it is necessary to accompany it with a 'micro-ecosystem' including nutrients and other stocks, natural or artificial. The chances of survival of these organisms in an ecosystem not managed by humans (agro-ecosystem or environments treated for pollution) would be slight by their very nature." (We may note here once again the indispensable contribution of a capacity to integrate the findings of research in the fields of molecular biology and ecology.)

R. COLWELL (Marine Biotechnology Center, Baltimore - ref.43), a specialist in microbial ecology, raises the question in the following terms: "Some scientists think that bacteria themselves effect genetic transfers, and r-DNA technology is only a reproduction of a natural process. The only difference lies in the 'speed' with which this process is realised through technology. What makes the **uncertainties** worrying is our lack of sufficient expertise in microbial ecology, i.e. the relationship of bacteria with other organisms. We only have a small amount of information relating to the dynamics of populations of new genotypes, placed in a new environment. But are these uncertainties any greater than in the past? No. However, the **demand for certainties** has grown because the public is becoming increasingly ignorant, and communication is getting difficult on account of a loss of confidence: the contradiction between different kinds of specialist expertise, poorly understood by the public, makes people lose confidence in science, and that confusion is undoubtedly the reason why the current regulatory framework exists."

From this point of view, it must be emphasised that the "ignorance" of the public is growing ever larger, in practical terms, because of progress in science, which is taking place with increasing rapidity and becoming increasingly restricted in its accessibility, given the growing specialisation of experts. What a scientist finds "uncertain" may in fact be situated within a "reassuring" framework, but that framework is not perceptible to a non- specialist public, and it is impossible for experts to communicate it. This raises the problem of integrating the progress of knowledge within society - rather than necessarily "accepting" it, which presupposes a contrast between "knowledge" and "culture".

IV.2.2 MICRO-ORGANISMS FOR POLLUTION TREATMENT

Micro-organisms are capable of **degrading** many types of chemical structure causing water, soil and atmospheric pollution. These capacities rely on the enzymatic equipment which they contain, and the natural environments are generally "enriched" by ecological processes of adaptation and selection of existing populations, into species which are capable of using the available substrata.

Traditional (biological) procedures for pollution treatment merely **favour** (by artificially modifying the physical and chemical parameters of sites, such as oxygenation, pH, nutrient concentrations) the biodegradation of substances contained in effluents by natural populations of micro-organisms.

But improved knowledge of the physiology and ecology of microbes also makes it possible to **modify these populations**, and, if the difficulty of resolving a given problem justifies the costs involved, to introduce "exotic" stocks of microbes, equipped with enhanced capacities for the degradation of pollutants, within the effluents to be treated. The potential activity represented by the natural (microbial) pool of genes is in fact a very major one - and as yet little understood.

Moreover, it is also possible to improve the performance of these stocks, by genetic mutation and selection of a "traditional" type, or through genetic engineering. These modifications should make it possible to make **pollutants "bio"-degradable which are not currently so**, thus enlarging the very concept of biodegradability or improving the ecological characteristics of pollutant treatment, when these are of a physical or chemical nature.

It is thought that more than 70,000 chemical substances are currently in use, scattered around various environmental areas. Some of these substances are believed to be dangerous, even toxic, for people, for domestic and wild fauna, for plants - or for micro-organisms of the soil.

The transformations of pollutants during biological procedures for effluent treatment take place **slowly**: there also exist possibilities of improving the speed of transformation of substrata by micro-organisms, by modifying or adapting their metabolism - either through traditional selection or through r-DNA genetic engineering.

The current **difficulties** found in implementing biotechnological procedures for treating pollution are of two kinds:

- few micro-organisms can **grow** in the presence of substrata in concentrations of the kind of ppb (parts per million) most frequently found in reality;

- our knowledge of their predators, and their **ecology** in general, is inadequate.

As for the **advantages** of biotechnological procedures, these are generally evaluated as follows:

- low investment costs
- low energy consumption
- self-performing operations
- opportunities for recovery (recycling).

The use of genetic engineering could help by enlarging the spectrum of application for biological procedures in damage control, making them more competitive. According to the American Federal Environmental Protection Agency, biological treatment of pollutants should be more *economical* than physical procedures (incineration).

A. Chakrabarty estimates that the activity of bacteria capable of degrading toxins can be increased through genetic engineering (for example, to treat 2, 4, 5 - T). In the United States, the number of toxic waste dump sites is estimated at 425,000. The cost of treating the most dangerous sites is estimated at 215 million dollars. The global market for these reclamation operations is estimated at **5 billion dollars per year between now and the year 2000**. At the present time, the (American) market for environmental biotechnology is estimated at 15 million dollars (in the form of microbial cultures).

Bacteria and yeasts using r-DNA will not represent a major part of these markets until about ten years have passed. The EPA is currently financing some research projects in this area, both with a view to using recombinant organisms themselves, and with a view to using the **enzymes** produced by these organisms. American companies like Ecova, Envirogen, Genencor, and General Electric are also said to be active in these areas of research.

The European Federation of Biotechnology (EFB) contains a working group given over to applications of biotechnology in the field of environmental improvement. The experts in this group (W. Verstraeten and E. Van Landuyt) believe that the use of r-DNA organisms is not possible in this sector, except where these organisms are matched by "micro-ecosystems" which allow them to function. These micro-ecosystems are made up of nutrients and other stocks which enhance or allow the recombinant organisms to get established in the places to be de-polluted. Other ways envisaged involve enzymes manufactured by recombinant organisms, but used "in vitro" to reclaim water, soils and atmosphere.

Some research in this field is concerned with the mobility of plasmids in soils or in water purification stations, with a view to determining the effectiveness of reclamation systems based on the use of plasmids with detoxifying characteristics. This approach offers the advantages of not using modified organisms, and of being patentable. But the mobility of these plasmids needs to be made better known, so that they can be prevented from propagating themselves in the environment in an inoperative and/or uncontrolled manner.

Biotechnology is also used to develop methods of evaluating the state of the environment ("**eco-diagnostics**"): immuno-assays are carried out with the help of reagents such as monoclonal antibodies for the detection of aromatic compounds, chlorated solvents, pesticides, and heavy metals. In Europe, the French "Lyonnaise des Eaux" company, for example, is perfecting a method for detecting dioxin, based on this principle.

The **success** of attempts to improve biological treatments for pollution will depend on:

- the possibilities of obtaining micro-organisms capable of **establishing themselves** in the areas to be treated;

- the possibilities for improving **speeds** of degradation;

- the possibilities for resolving problems inherent in the heterogeneous **spatial distribution** of pollutants, nutrients and micro-organisms.

A certain number of genes which are useful for xenobiotic degrading have been isolated from stocks present in contaminated soils, and are often located on plasmids (mostly in gram-negative bacteria, essentially Pseudomonas).

The first microbial stock which was patented (by A. Chakrabarty) in the United States had an enhanced capacity to break up chemical substances rarely found in the environment, but this stock has never been used in practice. (Unlike plasmids, natural stocks of micro-organisms cannot be patented as such.)

The **in vitro** production of new stocks requires a detailed knowledge of catabolic mechanisms, at a genetic and biochemical level. In the real world, the decontamination of sites by these stocks can be delayed or inhibited if the substratum inducing the degradation process is not present in sufficient quantity, or if the catabolism is inhibited by other substances. One of the possible ways of improving biological treatment procedures now seems to consist in enriching effluents with plasmids bearing genes which are useful for degradation. While this way also offers industry the advantage of being patentable, the possible risks associated with the mobility of these plasmids must be better analysed on a scientific level. This last point was indeed discussed in some detail at the seminar held in September 1991 (cf. Chapter V).

IV.3. ACCEPTANCE OF BIOTECHNOLOGY - INFLUENCE OF THE DEVELOPMENT OF APPLICATIONS IN THE ENVIRONMENT SECTOR

IV.3.1 COMMUNICATION

Some difficulties encountered by scientists and industrialists in securing an understanding and acceptance of the nature of their activities, and their ability to manage the risks associated with their implementation, illustrate the need to improve the opportunities for *interactive* communication between individuals faced with the development of science and technology. Consumers, for example, say that they not only wish to receive information, but also to have an opportunity to **express** their worries, fears, or hopes. The regulatory framework currently in place in Europe to control genetic engineering operations faces certain small and medium-sized firms with the impossibility of coping with administrative demands and presenting the dossiers needed to respond to numerous questions some of which are seen as pointless. Scientists see this as the outcome of an "enormous misunderstanding", arising from a breakdown in communication between "science" and "society"; some industrialists see it as the consequence of a lack of professionalism in the management of communication directed at public opinion, on the part of certain scientists (G. Boeken, PGS).

As often happens, entrenched positions are based on a simplistic view of the actors and problems involved. It must be pointed out that in certain cases, fortunately rare, there is an undeniable lack of commitment to transparent and interactive communication on the part of the potential information providers, the researchers and industrialists, and it must be recognised that there is also a lack of receptiveness, at times, on the part of certain "militants". The barrier of semantic difficulty is a constant one: some scientists willingly concede that they do not comprehend the totality of phenomena involved, and so they find it difficult to strike the right level of popularisation which would allow the recipients of the message to benefit from it. Although little information is available about the **scientific "culture"** of Europeans, the few existing studies show that we are better informed (globally) than American citizens, for example. Europeans also say that they are more interested (but see themselves as less well informed) in science and environmental problems than in politics and sport. Contrary to expectations, this shows that there are opportunities to improve the context of communication between science and society (Eurobarometer - W. Van Deelen - ref. 59).

We may note that within the Community, data concerning the Federal Republic of Germany deserve more detailed analysis. This is of course the part of Europe where **the ecological movement** has taken root, and shown the most violent opposition to industrialism and science-based development, whether this arises in connection with plans to install civil nuclear generating plants, or genetic engineering projects - two subjects which are not linked, however, either by their technological nature or by the importance and nature of the hazards which could conceivably emerge. But these are also the regions where the citizens questioned declare themselves **least** interested in the findings of scientific research, are among the most religious people in Europe, and perceive their institutions as being among the most democratic.

In the view of their opponents, the origins of certain excessive positions taken up by "ecological" movements are of an opportunist kind, and derive both from a certain conservatism (the refusal to change) and from dangerous simplification. While these excesses of a movement which is of relatively recent date and which, at times, is still looking for its own distinctive path, may be condemned, one has to see also that their positions express justified fears, a loss of confidence in science, and the legitimate desire for a "sustainable development", increased coherence between technical/scientific and industrial progress on the one hand, and the possibilities of preserving a planet which sustains and enhances life, on the other hand.

It must be admitted that these worries are often exacerbated by the presence of certain industrial developments which destroy resources and cause pollution, often resulting from the sometimes "untamed" industrialisation which took place at the beginning of the 20th century and the end of the 19th.

It will be necessary to reduce these excesses, and reconcile technical progress with rational ecological demands, while using the potential made available by innovative technologies in diminishing and remedying pollution. Such an approach, which is basically required by all actors, can only take place in a context of reassurance through balanced information which presents both sides of the argument, incorporating the findings from scientific projects of different kinds, including the findings from projects undertaken in the area of "bio-safety", for example, within the European BRIDGE programme.

The desire to be heard, which is sometimes expressed in an exaggeratedly combative style by interest groups, is yet another sign of the need for open dialogue. Only this can contribute to realism in decision-making, the effective implementation of decisions, and the democratic quality of the whole system.

As regards the understanding of the **concepts** of molecular biology and ecology, more precisely, the findings vary from one survey to the next - and although it is not certain that an improved understanding of these concepts leads to a better acceptance of biotechnology, the demand expressed, on the one hand, and the need to avoid neglecting any chance of improving the dialogue and the dynamism of a real democratic participation in our decisions on scientific development, on the other hand, presuppose that measures should be taken in favour of improvements in the provision of scientific information to the public. The answer to this difficulty may perhaps be found in the **communication of the true nature of the scientific approach** and the process of socio-economic development, more than in the communication of research findings.

The acceptability of biotechnology is negotiable at two levels: the decision in principle to become involved with this type of activity; and the objective determination of the risks connected with its use and the capacity to control them. Opinion surveys show that public attitudes regarding these two problems are based on different kinds of cultural components - only the second problem (concerning the existence of risks and their control) is accessible to negotiation and information. The first problem is connected with individual ideas about man and nature.

These ideas are, for many Europeans, anchored in ideas of a religious kind. In this connection, it may be pointed out that the World Council of Churches, for example, seems more understanding about the utilitarian concept of nature, prevalent in industrial countries, than about the possible attacks on the integrity and identity of the human genome (ref. 26).

This concern is undoubtedly a respectable one, and structures capable of ensuring the protection of the dignity of human beings must be consulted or set up. The religious authorities will have to be kept informed of progress in scientific knowledge, the effects of which may hopefully bring an improvement in the human condition in the social, economic and health fields - essential elements in the integrity and dignity of human persons - and place them in a position to assimilate this new knowledge as has happened in the past.

The **uncertainties** and the **contradictions** within the area of scientific expertise concerning the existence of environmental dangers of a new kind, associated with the use of r-DNA techniques, are felt to contribute to the loss of public confidence in the decision-making process. These contradictions (between specialists in molecular genetics and ecology, for example) will be resolved by enhanced interdisciplinary **integration** of research projects in the areas concerned. The departments of the Commission (DG XII) tend to favour dialogue between specialists in this connection. As for the ability of public opinion to deal with these uncertainties, Jacques

Monod, in *Le Hasard et la Nécessité (Chance and Necessity)*, explains that while it took on board the advantages offered by advances in knowledge, society has failed to realise that it was also necessary to make certain adjustments in our **beliefs** and our **judgements**. Scientific "truth", although in the eyes of real researchers it is a relative value which is subject to evolution, is unfortunately perceived (or presented) at times as a "revelation".

Despite its relative character, scientific and objective representation is becoming necessary more and more often to serve as one of the parameters of decision-making, in many fields. It sometimes happens that the uncertainties (and the necessity to evolve), which scientists perceive, are not borne in mind by those who apply scientific data in their decisions. The risk inherent in development based on our evolving knowledge remains low compared to the "natural" risks to which our ancestors were exposed: demographic facts are the best proof of this. It is no longer accepted to dream about an impossible and illusory 'zero' level of uncertainty. Such a "zero risk" could not be applicable anyway, without giving up the material progress of a rapidly growing world population.

On the other hand, the acceptance of **change** - and the risks associated with it - involves an ability to deal with uncertainties and, of course, a confidence in the institutions and in the economic and scientific actors involved in the development process.

The fact that a risk to which a large number of individuals are exposed **on a daily basis**, but which they have the impression of having chosen (such as driving a car or maintaining a smoking habit) is better "accepted" than the risks of accidents which are **improbable** but spectacular or novel, shows the extent to which emotional elements play a major role in determining individual attitudes. These attitudes result, on the one hand, from a desire to "master" the risks associated with changes in our lifestyle and the life of society, and on the other hand from a relative loss of confidence in the ability of institutions to protect individuals or in their consideration of the interests of populations exposed to risks when they are making their economic decisions. In this connection, an analysis and evaluation of the information made available to the public could, once again, be useful: sensational information is easy to sell, routine information is unsaleable (Ref. 4). Consequently, the public memory is better stocked with **sensational** events than with administrative and economic measures designed to contain technological risks. While it is "normal" to find the columns of daily newspapers telling of accidents and incidents of all kinds, it would be considered "indecent" to find these same newspapers providing a "defence" of institutions, science or industry, describing the efforts which are being made in order to contain risks (E. Yoxen, Scenarios for biotechnology in Europe).

S.C. Ehmig (Institut für Publizistik Johannes Gutenberg Universität) remarked, in the course of the "EC-US Task Force" programme on improving the communication of information on biotechnology (Dublin, March 1992) that in Germany the majority of general political journalists published "negative" stories on biotechnology. Although the scientific journalists make an effort to counterbalance these negative visions, their specialist pages are not read by the vast majority of newspaper readers.

It is felt by some people that the way in which information is communicated at the present time encourages not only a stabilisation but also a **sclerosis** in our societies, in the face of change. They observe, for example, that communiqués tend less and less to explain the reasoning and presuppositions leading to the conclusions of mediators, whose opinions are then taken as irrevocable. (This is the case, for example, with the headlines of articles in the printed media, which in many cases no longer contain verbs.) (Ref.4)

The **unilateral** character of mass communication by television - the most widely used by Europeans, an overwhelming majority of whom never open a scientific journal - can only engender a progressive indifference faced with the issues raised by our development. It is therefore possible that this "imposed conformism" may give rise to violent movements, such as those observed in certain regions with regard to biotechnology: **dialogue and information** represent the only alternative to showdowns and manipulation, in order to resolve these conflicts.

One example illustrating the difficulty of communicating an evaluation of technological development, and the importance of understanding the terms used and their impact, may be given here: scientists from the Wistar Institute in the USA had carried out trials of a recombinant bovine vaccine against rabies in Argentina without notifying the government of that country about the trials. This has been denounced as a scandal in the United States and Argentina. While the Argentinian government has complained about this (unacceptable) discourtesy on the part of the scientists, who had grown impatient on account of slow decision-making in the United States, documents produced by J.P. Lecocq (Transgène) nevertheless indicate that a commission of enquiry concluded that no evidence of damage to persons coming into contact with this vaccine had been established. On the other hand, a report published by the World Council of Churches ("Biotechnology, its Challenges to the Churches and the World") gives the impression (while the public is not unaware that rabies is a *fatal* disease) that 17 people were said to have had health problems through "contracting the disease". Information supplied by the European team of scientists who developed the vaccine indicates that contamination through a **recombinant** vaccine is **impossible**, as it is never pathogenic; that is indeed its main advantage by comparison with traditional vaccines. In fact, a recombinant vaccine is made up solely of molecules, their only effect on man being to trigger the desired immunological reaction. (The Higher Council of Churches has recognised this error of interpretation, and the vaccine is currently in use in a number of countries, having received administrative authorisations.

The scientific world cannot consider itself above the law and carry out illegal experiments; that much is obvious. The episode clearly indicates, however, that neither can it remain indifferent to the reactions of public opinion or the interpretations which are made of its work, and that researchers are also responsible for ensuring that their viewpoint is put forward on the mass media, so as to save the public from fearing the sinister consequences of technological change when such consequences are purely **imaginary**.

What has to be avoided is that the public wrongly "believes what it fears", and this must be done by informing public opinion - difficult though it may be - on the true workings of processes and the real content of products.

Scientists (and companies) must, in effect, conform to the regulatory needs of this complex process of information and decision-making, and this must happen whatever the "correctness" of the interpretation given to the nature of actual hazards by the decisions which are made.

As for individual attitudes in the face of technological risks, these attitudes are said to be made up of cognitive, emotional and behavioural elements. Opinions are developed on the basis of **heuristic** processes, sometimes involving the comparison of probabilities of the occurrence of events which have different natures and orders of causality; this may lead to distorted reasoning processes. Over-simplification and unjustified reductions of questions, fed by the absence of **comprehensible** information, may also lead to erroneous conclusions - which may indeed go in either direction. Lastly, interest and value components are sometimes lumped together by people **on both sides** of the information process .

Once their opinions have been formed, individuals no longer seem prepared to modify them, for example by taking on board supplementary information, except to the extent that this modification does not threaten their interests, their status or their position. The capacity of individuals to "question themselves" presupposes an adequate level of self-confidence, which can only be based on a far-reaching dialogue, not reduced to placing blind faith in technical and scientific progress, or to a sclerotic and obscurantist mental block when faced with innovation (Refs. 7, 8 and 12).

The **credibility** of information communicated to improve the level of public participation depends on the organisation or the personality of the chosen mediator. In certain cases, a similarity of "styles" between the mediator and the target population is desirable, while in other cases, the reputation, authority and competence of the mediator are more important. The confidence of individuals can also be more easily given to communications which present information in a comprehensive manner, but only a public which is sufficiently well informed is capable of coping with inherent contradictions (Ref. 12).

Communication strategies are thought to require three levels of design: the level of the practical problem (content), the level of semantics (language), and the level of effectiveness (targets). Information campaigns must take account of technical, cultural, ideological and institutional factors, which condition the possibilities of dialogue between protagonists. They should be defined in relation to clearly stated objectives, aiming at improving the level of participation. Their targets should be identified in terms of groups, attitudes and beliefs leading to fears which are without objective foundation. (Ref. 12).

Lastly, it could be added that the information given to the public should concern not only basic concepts of molecular biology and ecology, and the benefits which can be expected from the development of biotechnology, but also the nature of the scientific approach, the possible alternatives (and their consequences) to science-based development, the nature of the risks (whether speculative or actual) of accidents, and the socio-economic risks, their relative probability of occurrence, the technical and administrative measures to control the risks, and the measures taken to facilitate social and individual adaptation to change. It will therefore be necessary to remain attentive to the questionings of the public, and to respond to them, even when they appear irrational or unfounded.

Two examples of possible initiatives to improve dialogue concerning the implementation of biotechnology deserve to be cited here. These two examples come from Denmark - and it is not clear that these approaches can necessarily be transposed as they stand into other Member States, such is the extent to which they reflect the culture of that country. However, some lessons can certainly be drawn from the Danish experience.

Our first example is concerned with the organisation of "consensus conferences" (which, despite their name, are not designed to obtain a "consensus"). The objective pursued consists in improving information to *volunteer* members of the public: we are not dealing here with a negotiation between representatives of social groups or citizen organisations, nor with carrying out an opinion survey, as the findings have no statistical value, but rather what we have is the provision of an opportunity for representatives of the real "public" and experts to get together, to share information, and to draw up a "reference document" at the end of the exercise, which presents their different points of view. These points of view can then be used to provide information for members of Parliament about the preoccupations of a relatively well-informed public. It is on this basis, for example, that the Danish parliament limited allocation of public research funds for applications of genetic engineering to higher animals.

The second example, presented during the "Technology Assessment" symposium organised by FAST (EC DG XII) in Milan in November 1990, concerns a technology assessment project carried out by members of union organisations, especially laboratory technicians. This project, co-financed by these organisations and by the Danish Board of Technology, allowed the groups concerned to analyse their "job content" and to communicate the findings of their evaluation. Although one is dealing here with an "informed" and "involved" public, the conclusions of this evaluation were then communicated to a broader public. Such analyses cannot however be imposed - if they lose their voluntary character they also lose their legitimacy.

Similar evaluation processes are currently being carried out in Flanders (Belgium) by the STV (Stichting Technologie in Vlaanderen). In Italy, the Gramsci Institute (the Cultural Institute of the PDS, formerly the Italian Communist Party) is also organising a centre for bio-ethics, currently concerned with technologies providing medical assistance for procreation, research on the human genome, death and organ transplants.

Debates on the **socio-economic risks** associated with the development of biotechnology are clearer. The anticipated reinforcement of certain trends in the restructuring of industrial and agricultural sectors, for example, has given rise to strong opposition to the use of bovine growth hormones in the dairy sector. It can happen that the social groups concerned react to the innovations by opposing them, sometimes on the basis of health arguments. In this connection, some people feel that proposals aimed at explicitly introducing a fourth criterion (the socio-economic criterion) into the evaluation of the acceptability of new products have the advantage of making public positions more transparent, but others feel that they run counter to the European treaties, or indeed that they are unrealistic and impractical. Their merit resides mostly in the opportunity which they provide to distinguish and separate **conflicts of interest** from **conflicts of values** and **problems of safety**.

As for the **ethical questions** which certain people raise in relation to the application of genetic engineering techniques to livestock, for example, these questions must obviously be faced. A balanced approach to this area cannot ignore the comparison with traditional breeding practices of selection/hybridation. A group of members of the European Parliament including K. Collins, expressed a wish to set up a European Ethics Committee, the opinion of which could be sought on the occasion of certain uses of new technology. This committee has been established by the Commission, and not only will the Commission be able to consult it but it will also be able to take the initiative of expressing its views on cases where it believes that there are significant ethical aspects. In the opinion of most philosophers (such as M. Ruse, stated at a meeting of the International Bio-philosophy Forum - ref. 13)), such committees should not however be expected to provide *answers* to the questions which we might raise on "good" and "evil" - but we can expect them, rather, to define the *questions* to be posed. Answers will then have to be sought within the various available value- systems, presented by *philosophical* and *religious* groups. The ability to manage the ethical dimension of our socio-economic development could also require European institutions to re-think their modes of decision-making, while being careful to avoid unduly overburdening and slowing down a process which already seems cumbersome to many people.

This chapter on communication could be concluded with the following point: biotechnology based on molecular biology *modifies the way* in which people can improve living organisms which they use for economic ends, essentially by making this intervention more *"cognitive"* - and thus undoubtedly more *"responsible"*. Genetic engineering does not represent a new departure as regards the possibility of modifying biological evolution and ecosystems - but it has given us the new ability to carry out this modification with *greater understanding,* at the level of the molecular structure of living mechanisms; and this makes our way of relating to nature more transparent. Our society will probably have to learn to deal with this responsibility. What seems to scientifically minded people less risky - as the element of chance in our interventions decreases as our knowledge advances - can cause extra anxiety among those who do not understand this progress, or who lack confidence in the way in which this new "power" is used.

IV.3.2   PERCEPTIONS OF THE DEVELOPMENT OF APPLICATIONS OF BIOTECHNOLOGY IN THE ENVIRONMENTAL SECTOR

No study exists on this aspect of the acceptability of biotechnology. The Eurobarometer study set up by the departments of the Commission (DG XII CUBE) seems perhaps to indicate that this type of application is considered more acceptable than other ones, given the obvious advantages to everybody.

A certain number of experts have already been questioned on this subject, within the framework of the present project. However, it was not possible to hold interviews with the Commission officials in charge of European environmental policy.

In the United States, the "bio-remediation" sector (biological reclamation of old dump sites) is seen by the Environmental Protection Agency (**EPA**) as capable of improving the quality of the environment - this view is essentially concerned with the use of genetically manipulated micro-organisms, in conditions where their behaviour can be controlled. The director of this institution maintains this point of view, and encouraged the establishment of a working group to study conditions for development in this sector in March 1990. On the other hand, the **OTA** (the agency which assesses technological development for Congress) is currently studying the potential of the environmental bio-industry.

From an industrial point of view, the traditional American companies involved in the pollution treatment sector, and more specifically involved in the biological treatment of environmentally harmful substances, are hesitating to become involved openly in the application of genetic engineering, for two main kinds of reasons. The first kind of reason is connected with the extent of the costs of such developments, which cannot be borne by companies of a size which generally does not exceed ten people. The available expertise, built on microbial physiology and ecology, on the one hand, and on implementation techniques on the other hand, does not take in molecular biology.

The second type of reason has to do with anticipated problems of acceptance of new technology by those living near reclaimed sites, and the complexity of the administrative and technical measures which have to precede the issuing of permits. This reluctance has, in particular, led these companies to set up an association which is separate from the bio-industrial associations (such as ABC or IBA), called **ABTA** (Applied Biotreatment Association), which maintains an image resolutely separate from "bio-industry" and "biotechnology".

As for opinion groups, such as the National Wildlife Federation and the Friends of the Earth, their representatives believe that the existence of possibilities for using biotechnology to remedy environmental problems cannot be used either to justify activities which cause pollution, nor to accelerate the use of genetically manipulated organisms without special controls. These groups, just like the representatives of the pollution treatment industry, are favourable to the development of the bio-remediation market through the passing of more stringent laws to improve the quality of the environment, or through the freeing of government funds to reclaim old toxic waste dumps. (The EPA has in fact freed "superfunds" for this purpose for a number of years. It should be noted that the majority of sites designated for priority reclamation belong to federal agencies such as the Energy Department or the Defence Department. Most of them are not domestic or industrial sites.)

The European experts neither expressed nor perceived a radical opposition to the use of r-DNA micro-organisms for pollution treatment, so long as appropriate methods of physical or biological containment are used, and "risks" are controlled. To the extent that these conditions can be fulfilled, biotechnological procedures for pollution treatment can generally be perceived as more acceptable from an ecological point of view than physical procedures such as incineration. However, the position of the more radical representatives from the environmentalist groups is that, on the one hand, it should not be necessary to undertake pollution treatment, and on the other hand that pollution treatment procedures should no longer be content with "shifting the problems somewhere else";

lastly, they feel that it should no longer be necessary to develop "more technologies" to repair the damage caused by our mode of development.

IV.3.3 PERCEPTIONS OF THE STRATEGIES OF LARGE COMPANIES WITHIN THE PLANT HEALTH SECTOR

One of the initial strategies used by the chemical industry consisted in integrating the plant breeders' sector and developing seeds, for example, resistant to **herbicides**, with a view to improving the possibility of managing vegetable crops.

This strategy was denounced, notably by J. Doyle (Friends of the Earth), R. Goldberg (Environmental Defence Fund), and M. Mellon (National Wildlife Federation), on the grounds that it must necessarily lead to an increase in the quantity of herbicides being used in agriculture. The scientific experts who were consulted thought that this view was exaggerated, and felt on the contrary that such strategy will make it possible to use herbicides of a new kind, less harmful to the environment, in smaller quantities. In any case, in industrialised countries, the institutions charged with protecting the environment control the use of these products.

The development plans of chemical companies and small genetic engineering firms also involve products based on the **inverse strategy** - such as plants resistant to insects or diseases, and biopesticides. Some of the scientists we spoke to also mentioned some possibilities in this area which have not yet been explored, such as moulds equipped with herbicidal capacities. In this connection it would be useful to evaluate in more detail the extent to which market conditions favour the development of eco-specific solutions to pest control and the control of crop diseases, meaning strategies for diversifying systems for managing agro-ecosystems, rather than large-scale production of a uniform kind which leads to uniformity.

On the development of plants equipped with genes resistant to insects, such as the Bacillus Thuringiensis gene, J. Doyle remarks that there is a risk of engendering a **resistance** of insects to BT, just like the emergence of insects resistant to chemical insecticides. The molecular biologists reply that it is already possible to obtain a diversified range of BT genes, and that while resistances are inevitable, the fight against pests is nonetheless a necessary one.

M. Mellon suggests that the improvement in the environment in the agricultural sector can never be achieved so long as the strategies pursued by chemical companies are limited to offering solutions in terms of products, and not in terms of systems for managing agro-ecosystems, bearing in mind the diversity of local ecological conditions, and the contributions of traditional farming in terms of know-how.

She remarks more pragmatically that the largest American chemical company in the plant health sector, which employs eight hundred people in developing biotechnology, appears to have no expert in plant ecology, and that the entire strategy is thus essentially shaped by the vision of molecular biology. (It was not possible to verify this.)

In this connection we may observe that strategy *is already* showing signs of evolving towards "systems" rather than (chemical) "products", given that current research is concentrating on the development, for example, of *seeds* with improved potential - and that the success of this research will depend essentially on how well these seeds adapt to the environments where they are to be planted.

Some representatives of the European environmentalist groups (P. Lannoye) are also convinced that the majority of R & D projects in companies in the chemical sector are orientated towards the production of plants which are resistant to herbicides, with the aim of increasing the sale of chemical products in agriculture. It is difficult to obtain reliable information on this topic: by way of example there follows a table drawn up by the GIBIP (Green Industry Biotechnology Information Platform) industrial association.

The list of projects financed within European biotechnology programmes mentions no project in this area. (cf. "European Laboratory without walls" - E. Magnien - D. de Nettancourt - EC - DG XII - 1991).

This does not mean that projects intended to develop herbicide-resistant plants are not being implemented - but that there are also **other** approaches to research, and that these possibilities are also being explored by industry and scientists.

SURVEY RESULTS
on Biotech Research Allocation
by GIBIP members

	Research area	Average resource allocation (proportion of R&D Investment)
1.	Improved breeding technologies	35 %
2.	Disease resistance	21 %
3.	Product Quality modification	14 %
4.	Herbicide tolerance	13 %
5.	Insect tolerance	9 %
6.	Stress tolerance	3 %
7.	Others (yield, etc.)	n.a.

(Consolidated total from 16 members)

IV.4. BIOTECHNOLOGY AND SUSTAINABLE DEVELOPMENT

"**Sustainable development**" is a concept proposed by the Environment Development Commission of the United Nations, in the report published in 1987 under the title of "The Brundtland Report". It is an attempt to reconcile economic growth with the objectives of environmental quality for developing countries as well as industrialised countries. Sustainable development is thus a process of economic growth which is capable of resolving social problems, but is "tolerable" in terms of preserving the biosphere's capacity for reproduction.

Many experts are now concentrating on questions connected with the establishment of **criteria** for evaluating the "sustainability" of economic activities and technologies. These questions involve economic and ecological calculations, environmental balance-sheets and the actualisation of costs for current removal of environmental resources from future generations, on the one hand, and the integration of economic and ecological objectives by organisations, institutions, companies, technologies and individuals, on the other hand.

The **comparative** evaluation of "sustainability" and the social acceptability of production types and technologies will be attainable once ecological costs have been taken on board by the economy. From that point onwards, consumers will in fact be able to make choices on the basis of real global costs, about which products they judge most appropriate to satisfy their needs, on the basis of clearly established criteria resulting from compromises between the public interest, individual interests, the interests of future generations and those of the biosphere.

These globalised visions must not however obscure the practical reality: products produced by activities which have an added cost because of compliance with "environmental" regulations run the risk, at the margin, of placing themselves outside the reach of groups with a small income.

An evaluation of the "sustainability" of bio-industrial activities is currently hard to achieve. We have found no original analysis in this regard, most current positions being essentially based on **a priori** assessments, especially given the absence of "objective" criteria to form a basis for judgement.

In the current state of affairs, only international companies in the chemical sector, established in most of the key sectors such as human and animal health, agriculture, energy and even the environment, can command the *competences*, the *expertise* and the *resources* to secure a transition from our way of economic development towards a "sustainable" type of development, both in the developing countries and in the industrialised world. Neither the institutions (national or international), nor the opinion groups, nor the economic actors who are committed to one or other particular sector, will be capable of achieving this change. But in the logic of our economy, this mutation will only be achieved if **market conditions** - meaning not only regulations but also consumer preferences, and thus also the way in which they are informed - are favourable to such development. In this connection, the restructuring which could be expected to follow the internalisation of ecological costs could give rise to new types of social problems, which - to the best of our knowledge - have not been subjected to serious analysis.

Bio-industrial development and the use of biotechnology result from accumulated progress of knowledge in the various areas of **life sciences.** While the accent has often been placed on the contribution of molecular biology, progress has also been achieved in other areas, such as physiology, ecology and the pathology of living species - and it is the **integration** of findings in all of these disciplines together which makes technological innovation possible, when the corresponding markets exist. Biotechnology, emerging from an improved capacity to understand life and used to satisfy the needs expressed by the market, should therefore be able to permit a more "sustainable" level of economic development, by "nature".

While the conditions for the use of living beings (micro-organisms, vegetables and animals) for economic ends remain perhaps to be defined or negotiated between different people's sensitivities with regard to nature, and while the notion of "risks to the environment" remains to be defined in the case of genetic engineering, biotechnology offers the possibility of **"negotiating with nature"**, while preserving its capacity for reproduction and the interests of our own species, the conditions of an economic development which "integrates" ecological objectives. But such evaluations of the comparative sustainability of different types of production are not available.

J.F. Bunders, of the University of Amsterdam, has assessed the conditions for the application of biotechnology for "sustainable development" in the developing countries. Her analysis was published in *Biotechnology for small-scale farmers in developing countries*, published by the University Press of the Free University of Amsterdam in 1990. This is essentially an analysis of the way in which biotechnology should be integrated into the local development process of non-developed countries, and the conditions of economic profitability for the use of "eco-local" solutions for the least favoured farmers in these countries.

The representative of the National Farming Research Institute of Zimbabwe expressed the opinion, at the FAST Technology Assessment symposium organised in Milan in 1990, that "no type of biotechnology will be usable by small farmers unless it is developed on the basis of an analysis of their farming traditions, on the one hand, and the ecological conditions under which their current techniques are operated". This approach is also seen as necessary to assure a sustainable development of agriculture in these countries through biotechnology.

As regards the assessment of the extent to which "biotechnological" agriculture is more "sustainable", from an ecological point of view, than "industrial" agriculture, the following questions have to be asked:

1) Is it possible to feed the population of the world through "biological" agriculture (meaning "organic" and extensive, without technological help)?
If the response to this question is negative:

2) Can "biotechnological" agriculture be considered as "more sustainable" than "chemical" agriculture?
If the response to this question is positive:

3) Under what conditions can "biotechnological" agriculture improve the condition of farmers and consumers in developing countries and in industrialised countries?

4) Under what conditions can agriculture develop by adapting different types of production to local eco- conditions, and how can the development of biotechnology contribute to this diversification? What are the market conditions which can direct the strategies of major companies in this direction?

The notion of "sustainable" economic development implies that economic activities should take account, in their way of utilising natural resources, of the limits set by the biosphere's capacity for reproduction.

Among recent developments in the bio-industrial domain, one may cite some examples of the use of the capabilities of living organisms for this purpose:

1) Development (through genetic engineering) of stocks of yeast which can cut pollution by beer-producing breweries (ALKO, Finland)

2) Genetic modification of plants with a view to decreasing the need to use pesticides

3) Biological counter-measures and biopesticides in agriculture

4) Production of therapeutic substances through the genetic engineering of micro-organisms, replacing the use of chemical procedures and of synthetic chemical products.

But the "economic truth" will only be perceptible when the cost of products manufactured by different types of production begin to reflect the internalisation of pollution treatment costs, following the application of the (European) principle of "the polluter pays".

IV.5. THE POLITICAL AND REGULATORY FRAMEWORK OF THE ENVIRONMENTAL BIO-INDUSTRY

The possibilities of developing applications of biotechnology in the environmental sector are essentially conditioned by two types of policies and regulations, which we shall analyse at EC level.

The first group of regulations and policies is concerned with the protection of the environment, against the effects of industrial and agricultural activities. These policies "create" the markets for reclamation and bio-remediation, or, more recently, the market for clean technology. Whether from the point of view of agricultural production or industrial production, one may reflect that European policy on the environment has been evolving, between 1972 and the present day, towards a greater integration of environmental objectives within economic decision-making. The Community's first environmental action plan (1972) consisted essentially of a set of measures designed to **correct** the effects of economic development on ecosystems and health. Later, preventive measures (such as the directive on the risks of major accidents, or the directive on impact studies) were put in place. The Agricultural Policy also contains provision for compensation payable to farmers using techniques which are not competitive but could help to preserve the environment.

Since 1986, however, the Single European Act (Title VII, Articles 130 R, S, T) provides explicitly that pollution treatment costs must be **internalised** (the "polluter pays" principle) and that environmental policies should be **integrated** as a component of other policies. This has led to the establishment, within the departments of the Commission for example, of a certain number of interdepartmental working groups, or the holding of "mixed" European Councils, such as the Council on "Energy and Environment" or "Development and Environment". Finally, since the Rome Council meeting, the political will to use **economic and fiscal instruments** in environmental policies was expressed, and, following the Council meeting in Dublin, the need to promote an environmental **ethic** in Europe has emerged (P. Bourdeau, DG XII).

The second group of policies is represented by regulations specifically concerned with biotechnology and the bio- industry.

Different analyses or criticisms of these regulations have been published or expressed - and these criticisms are summarised at the beginning of the report. There is a certain inconsistency in these regulations which may appear incompatible with the imperatives of a "holistic" or "global" approach, recommended by not only most of the specialists in environmental sciences, to ensure our transition towards what some people call "sustainable development", but also, since the passing of Article 130 R, S, T of the Single European Act, by the European Treaties.

It will undoubtedly be necessary to review, in a more global and more balanced perspective - and perhaps in a broader international framework - all existing regulations (or the absence of regulations) and the procedures for assessing a "redefined biological risk". This review should concern *all* economic activities which modify the gene pools of ecosystems and agro-ecosystems, ranging from traditional agricultural selection procedures to the techniques of molecular biology. The objective bases needed for this fundamental reassessment are probably not as inaccessible as is sometimes stated at the present time (National Research Council, USA). This assessment could be entrusted to specialists in ecology, agronomy, molecular biology, genetic engineering, classical genetics and "environmental sciences". On the lines of what is being done within the EPA (USA) or the OECD, it is necessary that this problem should be tackled in Europe in as objective a setting as possible, without singling out r-DNA techniques as elements which provoke unreasoning passions.

The aims of this assessment procedure could be as follows:

1) To identify and compare the dangers (actual and conjectural) to ecosystems represented by the introduction of "exotic" organisms (natural or modified), and objective decision-making criteria regarding the acceptability of such introductions.

2) To make a rigorous analysis of the possible existence of potential risks which could be objectively and specifically linked with the use of r-DNA techniques in relation to the risks caused by the use of other types of organisms (pathogens for one species or another, for example) in traditional agricultural and industrial activities, which are covered, or uncovered, by current regulations.

3) To consider the social, economic and ecological **advantages**, as well as the dangers (actual and conjectural) of the possible development of biotechnology; this should lead to an integrated, or more integrated, approach to decision-making as regards hazard control. In this connection it should be recalled that the Commission has set up, within DG XII, a "Co-ordination Unit for Biotechnology in Europe" (CUBE), but the influence of this unit on decision-making practices has unfortunately remained limited, because it is part of one of the Directorates- General within the departments of the Commission.

In addition, more recently, an attempt to integrate various parameters was carried out through the establishment of the BCC (Biotechnology Co-ordination Committee) within the Secretariat General (cf. VI.1.4).

One should also note the recent establishment of a "Committee for the Ethics of Biotechnology Applications" in Europe.

Lastly, one may note the publication by the American government (Federal Register, 27/2/92) of a new approach to regulations designed to control hazards linked with the use of organisms produced by genetic engineering in the environment: this approach allows for deregulation where hazards are non-existent.

V. THE SEMINAR IN DUBLIN, 2 - 4 SEPTEMBER 1991

V.I OBJECTIVES

A first report of "findings" covering the topic of this research project (cf. Chapter IV) was delivered at the end of 1990. The Foundation then decided to have this preliminary document debated by a group of experts, chosen in particular among those people who had been questioned during the survey.

This preliminary survey was in fact drawn up at the point when genetic engineering, the technology which could be seen as central in the development of a competitive bio-industry, was being subjected to major debates within European decision-making circles, especially in the environmental sector. There was thus a risk that the survey process might have been set in motion either too early or too late for those people in charge of the policies involved, who should have been questioned, to make themselves available and contribute to the preparation of a balanced synthesis from all points of view.

This explains why certain authorities, whether administrative or political (such as the representatives of DG XI), who were contacted for the compilation of the report on findings, were not in fact available for interview.

The seminar was thus given the particular task of completing the information which had been presented in the report of findings, and filling in certain gaps.

The question posed by this process of survey and reflection concerns in particular the market for applied genetic engineering in the treatment of harmful waste products, and, more broadly, the evaluation and perception of the possible impact of the products of genetic engineering on the environment.

What is henceforth called the "environment market" is essentially conditioned by the demand created by the regulations which determine the quality objectives for the environment - whatever the "degree of cleanliness" in future production procedures.

In this connection, a complete and forward-looking range of information on the policies and priorities of the authorities charged with protecting the environment in Europe was indispensable. The "Action Plan for the Environment" of the Commission, covering the period 1987- 1992, contained in particular a heading entitled "Best use of biotechnology".

As regards the policy of developing biotechnology, the Commission published in April 1991 a communication on promoting the competitiveness of bio-industry in the Community (SEC (91) 629).

These two declarations of principle provide the starting point from which socio-economic actors must draw their strategies for developing applications of genetic engineering in the environmental sector. But the interpretation of these principles remains largely a matter of chance, and that is why an interview, for example with those in charge of environmental protection policies in the area of biotechnology, would have been useful.

The evaluation of the acceptance of products and techniques by consumers and by the "public" constitutes an important part of market studies. The success of a given technology is in fact conditioned by its competitiveness, its development and application costs, its specific features and advantages in relation to the objectives pursued, but also by its public acceptance, which is notably influenced by the perception of risks (or uncertainties) associated with its implementation. These perceptions in turn may condition the context within which technology develops, i.e. the political and regulatory framework. On this topic, it is important to note that while restrictive regulations are theoretically capable of reassuring the public, and thus improving the acceptability of technology, when these constraints are exaggerated by comparison with the real levels of risk, not only do they sacrifice the competitiveness of agents of innovation (companies and scientists), but they also contribute to reinforcing the perceptions whereby these technologies are felt to be "dangerous" - and a vicious circle which runs against everybody's interests is thereby set up.

The discussion of these aspects during the seminar was organised under five topics:

1	Scientific bases
2	Technological considerations and R&D policy
3	Socio-economic, industrial and financial considerations
4	Political and public opinion questions
5	Regulations

Five groups of *"key questions"* had been presented to participants, providing the framework for the discussions.

The people invited had been selected particularly among the people contacted during the enquiry stage, and represented the scientific world (7), institutions (16), industry (12) and opinion groups or interest groups (13).

(The list of participants is given in Annex V.)

V.2 REPORT

The report of this seminar is divided into three parts:

1 A summary of the *evaluation* of the "report of findings";

2 An *updating* of information (events which took place since December 1990);

3 A *summary of the responses* given to the "key questions" during the seminar.

V.2.1 EVALUATION OF THE "REPORT OF FINDINGS"

Some participants observed that the report gave a great deal of importance to genetic engineering, whereas these techniques were not yet seen as essential to ensure the development of biological treatment of pollution. In response to this observation, our response is that, as with all sectors of bio-industry (defined as those production activities which use living organisms or certain of their constituents), the bio-industrial pollution treatment sector is affected, in the medium and long term, in the area of **competitiveness**, by the possibilities of using innovative techniques, such as for example those techniques which consist in improving the organisms used, especially by the use of genetic engineering.

Apart from that comment, the main thrust of the report was not criticised.

V.2.2 UPDATING OF THE REPORT (EVENTS SINCE 1990)

V.2.2.1 Biotechnology Co-ordination Committee (BCC)

With a view to strengthening co-ordination between the positions and provisions of the various Directorates General within the Services of the Commission, the "BCC" was put in place, starting in 1991, under the ægis of the Secretariat General.

On the basis of this initiative, one may reasonably hope to see European policies proceeding, in the matter of biotechnology, towards a better **integration** between social, ethical, consumer and environmental considerations.

The Commission document published in April 1991 (SEC (91) 629), resulting from a preliminary attempt to present integrated views on the preservation of the competitiveness of the European bio-industry, contains in particular references to the opportunities offered by biotechnology in the environmental sector. It also contains indications as to the possible development of regulations, with these regulations being updated on the basis of accumulated experience in the area of the scientific evaluation of hazards.

V.2.2.2 IRRO - Information Resource on the Release of Organisms in the Environment

During two meetings, held in March 1991 in Vienna, and in August 1991 in Nottingham, with support notably from UNEP and the EC, a decision was taken to improve access at world level to information concerning the ecological impact of living organisms introduced into the environment.

A network of access to existing databanks, or those currently being set up, facilitating the retrieval of information covering the impact of organisms both natural and modified (particularly by means of genetic engineering) was thus put in place by the MSDN (Microbial

Strain Data Network). A greater availability of this type of information will make it possible to evaluate the environmental impact of genetic engineering, in a realistic perspective - i.e. by comparison with other techniques which introduce foreign organisms into a given environment.

This seems to indicate that there is a will, at least within the scientific community, to improve the "rationality" of the approach adopted in these areas.

V.2.2.3   **OECD - CPST project concerned with "bioremediation"**

The CPST("Comité de Politique Scientifique et Technologique" - Science and Technology Policy Committee) is currently preparing a report on biotechnology in the environmental sector, which ought to become available in 1993.

V.2.2.4   **The Dublin Foundation - report prepared by L. Lemkow (Barcelona) and debated during a seminar organised in Madrid in May 1991: "Public Opinion and Biotechnology"**

This project is concerned with the evaluation of survey projects relating to the perceptions of biotechnology - and more particularly genetic engineering - by European societies. The essential point that it brings out is the major **divergence** between these perceptions, and the fundamental differences which exist in this connection between different regions of the Community.

V.2.2.5   **EC - DG XII (CUBE): Eurobarometer - Public opinion survey covering biotechnology in the EC**

This survey, based on the questioning of 12,000 people in the Community, seems to suggest in particular that an improvement in public information might improve the level of acceptance for technology.

The use of biotechnology to improve the impact of our activities on the environment seems on the other hand to be considered "acceptable" by the majority of Europeans.

V.2.2.6   EPA (USA) - "Bioremediation Action Committee"

The activities of this Committee, set up in 1990, are designed to support the development of applications for biotechnology to improve the treatment of harmful wastes, and more generally, to enhance **communication** between this Agency and bio-industry. So far, no application of manipulated organisms has been carried out - although it is possible that this could be envisaged in the future.

One of the preoccupations of this working group (which also includes representatives from American associations for the defence of the environment) consists notably in overcoming the obstacles to the development of "innovative" technologies which in most current specifications (which order the use of the "best available technologies") are placed in an unfavourable position, by comparison with techniques which have been better tested by the state of the art, such as incineration, for example.

With a view to encouraging the implementation of showpiece projects, on a small scale, permits are issued in the bioremediation field.

V.2.2.7   The point of view of developing countries - UNCSTD - UNIDO

We had not included any interviews on this topic in the "findings" report. A representative of UNIDO pointed out the danger represented both by "over-regulated" zones and by "uncontrolled" zones, for developing countries. Given the relationship of interdependence between the countries of the North and the South, the development of regulatory policies in developing countries must be taken into account. Excessively strict regulations lead to bureaucracies gaining control, and these bureaucracies (as has already happened) will lead certain companies to carry out their trials where no regulations yet exist, in the absence of sufficiently clear and prompt decisions in the industrialised countries. Similarly, the absence of control measures may inhibit technology transfer. The need to prepare a regulatory approach which is accepted, at international level, by all the zones of economic influence, for exchanges of products and biotechnological procedures, is clearcut.

In this connection, reference has been made to the work carried out by UNIDO aimed at establishing a (voluntary) international code of good conduct relating to the diffusion of genetically manipulated organisms in the environment. International agreements should contain clear and unequivocal criteria, allowing any government to decide whether to issue or refuse permits and licences. The exchange of information relating to the findings of trials carried out for different types of organism, in different types of ecosystems, and in different kinds of conditions, should also be improved (see IRRO).

N.B. On this same subject, since the seminar held in Dublin to discuss the present report, mention must also be made of the preparatory documentation for the Rio "World Summit" conference (organised in June 1992 by UNCED), and the documents from the United Nations which state that the technology of genetic engineering is neither "intrinsically dangerous nor intrinsically free of danger", on the one hand, and on the other hand, insisting on the need, for developing countries, to have access to biotechnology to *improve* the condition of the environment.

V.2.3 RESPONSES TO KEY QUESTIONS

Topic I   **The basis of scientific knowledge**

Questions:

1.1:   What is the scientific base of current knowledge for the development of genetically manipulated organisms in pollution treatment and bioremediation?

1.2:   What is the current experimental base: does the addition of plasmids represent a viable solution?

1.3:   What is the potential contribution which biotechnology could make to improve the procedures for pollution treatment currently in use?

1.4:   What are the possible risks linked to the use of genetically manipulated organisms in water purification plants, in the treatment of toxic waste storage sites or dumps, and for fuel spillages? Do these uses constitute confined utilisations, or applications in the environment?

Summary of responses:

- The current knowledge base allows expectations that the concept of "biodegradability" can be effectively enlarged, particularly due to genetic engineering of micro-organisms (essentially bacteria).

- These prospects must not, however, allow us to think of being able to throw pollutant substances freely into the environment, nor can we neglect the evaluation of possible environmental or health impacts of organisms introduced through pollution treatment procedures. This impact must be evaluated, whether one is dealing with natural or modified bacteria, by genetic engineering or other procedures.

- The currently available experimental basis in the bioremediation field, using genetic engineering, is still limited for a whole range of reasons, but should in any case be made better known to the public.

- The European experience is developing in this area, notably in the framework of the "biosecurity" portion of the European BRIDGE programme.

- While the addition of plasmids bearing characters which equip organisms with new biodegrading capabilities represents a possible line of investigation, a more promising line consists in modifying the bacteria which are native to the sites to be cleaned up: this procedure minimises the proportion of "uncertainties" introduced by our intervention in the natural processes of adaptation, selection and evolution of natural species (R. Colwell).

- The potential contribution of biotechnology and genetic engineering to improve current pollution treatments is a real one, but it must be quickly demonstrated by convincing results. These must be conveyed to the public through a major publicity campaign.

- The merit of biological procedures, by comparison with other pollution treatment procedures, could be better validated by comparing the total uses of energy and final impacts on the environment. The difficulty in this area comes from the absence of "objective" criteria for evaluation in a sufficient quantity. But the European Biotechnology Federation and the EPA are already of the opinion that in some cases, biological procedures would be more advantageous, from both an economic and an ecological point of view, especially if one compares them to incineration.

- The (conjectural) risks associated with the use of genetically modified micro-organisms in pollution treatment have been mentioned, notably by P. Schenkelaar, D. Dwyer and R. Colwell. It would, incidentally, be appropriate to talk of "uncertainties" rather than "dangers". These uncertainties become more significant as the gap between known situations and new situations grows wider.

- The perception of "dangers" by the public seems to be essentially bound up with the use of microbial agents (bacteria) in these applications: this was shown by the bioremediation experiments (stimulation of growth of native non-manipulated bacteria in Alaska - Exxon Valdez, EPA).

- The utilisation of genetically manipulated organisms in water purification facilities would involve fewer uncertainties than their use in procedures for cleaning up land and water tables. Experience shows that there are biological containment procedures which can guarantee a 99% disappearance of the modified organisms introduced into the environment, after they have fulfilled their purpose. On the other hand, modified metabolisms can be selected in such a way as to mineralise the degraded substances completely, avoiding the production of secondary toxic metabolites. It is also necessary to choose the induced characteristics in such a way as to stop them from allowing bacteria to degrade substances which are "resources" rather than "waste products".

- As regards the uncertainties linked to the utilisation of modified organisms by molecular biology techniques, the representatives of the scientific world have emphasised the fact that, in order to obtain these modifications, it is necessary to "understand" them so fully that uncertainties are reduced to a minimum.

- Finally, in most cases, it is necessary to supplement the introduced bacteria with nutrients, and the disappearance of those nutrients, after the organisms have purified the sites, prevents the populations of "exotic" organisms from establishing themselves in the longer term.

- Similarly, once the specific substrata of the introduced organisms have disappeared, their population also disappears.

- The scientists generally use several types of biological containment, along these lines, to ensure the safety of the procedures which are used.

- But disagreements between experts will never be completely resolved (that is the very nature of the scientific approach): some participants (P. Schenkelaar) recommend, in order to counteract these disagreements, that "peer evaluations" of the different expert views should be organised.

Topic II   Considerations of technology and R&D policy

Questions:

2.1:   What are the R&D priorities for public institutions such as the EC or for industry?

2.2:   What are the needs in terms of developments in procedures, reactors, etc.?

2.3:   How to obtain better interdisciplinary integration and better communication between molecular biology and ecology?

2.4:   What are the links between these questions and the more general questions concerning the economy of the environment and the research programmes implemented in environmental science, for example within the framework of European programmes?

Summary of responses:

- A certain number of R&D priorities were given, which were concerned both with molecular biology in the strict sense and with the physiology and ecology of microbes or engineering sciences (implementation procedures).

- The importance of having the resources to finance pilot activities beyond the initial R&D phase was also brought out.

- Certain opinion groups would also wish to have funds not only to inform the public, but also to carry out alternative trials which would allow them to evaluate, confirm or disprove the findings of trials carried out by the industry or by the authorities.

- The need for a constant improvement in our knowledge base (in all the areas concerned) was stressed notably by Professor Oliveira, who recalled that "the Universe does not forgive us our ignorance".

- The importance of an interdisciplinary approach was also emphasised. This should be supplemented by a "global" (or more global) approach as regards the evaluation of the ultimate impact of pollution treatment processes on the environment.

- The example of the projects implemented within the framework of the "biosecurity" portion of the BRIDGE programme and within the STEP programme (environment sciences research) has already been mentioned. Similarly, the EUREKA programme provides a framework for the development of new techniques for pollution treatment and "clean" (or "cleaner") production procedures. However, no new suggestions for interdisciplinary actions were formulated by the expert group.

- Links with research projects on the economy of the environment, which are to be implemented within the new European R&D programme on the environment could usefully be established.

- The representatives of the trade union organisations recalled their demand that European technological R&D budgets should include a 10% allocation to carry out studies covering "technology assessments", or evaluations of the socio-economic impacts of scientific and technological developments. Up to the present time, at European level, such evaluations were essentially carried out within the framework of the MONITOR programme (SAST and FAST). The extent of the budgets for these programmes certainly falls short of 10% of the budgetary amounts allocated to scientific and technological research in Europe, but on the other hand, 10% of the current framework programme is given over to research in the environmental area.

Exploratory research in technology assessment is being established particular under the umbrella of the FLAIR programme.

- The representatives of industry stressed the fact that these technological evaluations are much more hazardous, and their findings much less certain and reliable, than those obtained through "scientific" research (one is dealing with forecasts and "scenarios"). They must be implemented and assessed with a great deal of intelligence, taking account of contradictory views, and must not tempt institutions to orientate their development by introducing criteria other than the three traditional scientific ones (safety, quality and efficacy).

- On the other hand, as was made clear by one representative from the OTA (Office of Technology Assessment of the American Congress), the choice facing a government in this area, on the basis of the findings from these studies, consists either in banning a given technology which is felt to be capable of causing unacceptable structural modifications, or else in laying down accompanying measures, allowing individuals and organisations (including economic actors suffering a disadvantage, such as farmers, in some cases for example) to participate more fully in the changes - i.e. developing themselves within their own structures, their aspirations, their objectives, their motivations, their competences, etc.

- The need to evolve, whatever the technological circumstances, was mentioned by a certain number of participants, and the blocking measures aimed at certain technological developments were criticised as possible indicators of a refusal of innovations which are necessary to adapt our societies to unstoppable developments in the "natural" and "socio-economic" environment (if only in its demographic aspect). This necessity could be more effectively communicated to the public - and could lead to complementary measures of an institutional kind making these changes more "acceptable".

> **Topic III**   **Economic, industrial and financial considerations**

Questions:

3.1   What are the current projections concerning the economic viability of environmental bio-industries? What are the investments in this sector?

3.2:   How can the markets for these companies be developed by European institutions?

3.3:   How can the biological portion of these markets be extended, and what role can the EC play in this connection?

3.4:   What improved incentives could be provided for this sector?

Summary of responses:

- These questions gave rise, in the first place, to a discussion about the very existence of an "environmental market", or concerning the need, the possibility or the desirability to translate environmental protection needs into economic terms. These divergences lead one to think that research on the economy of the environment, envisaged in the new European programme of environmental R&D, is even more necessary. A certain number of responses, in terms of new definitions and concepts, and in terms of the development of a conceptual reference framework, making it possible, as suggested in the Brundtland report, to achieve a better **integration** between environmental and economic considerations, could be provided by these research projects. They could also be usefully applied to a more objective assessment of the impact of biotechnology on the environment - or of the conditions within which these applications could be judged acceptable.

- Some experts confirmed that this is a difficult and uncertain market, in the absence of clear and transparent policies, both in the area of bio-industrial development and in the area of environmental protection.

- While there is no formal association of companies in this sector, the representative from the EUREKA programme felt that the network of companies participating in the EUROENVIRON project could, in some ways, be considered as such an association.

- Some experts confirmed that this market is essentially conditioned by the regulations on environmental protection.

- Given the special difficulties in this sector and the importance of the environmental problems, stronger support from European institutions is desirable, both from those in charge of R&D policy and from those with responsibilities for environmental and industrial policies.

- No new practical suggestions on incentives which could be used in this sector was put forward, apart from the maintenance of pilot projects. This need is not always understood or admitted by the representatives of environmental protection groups, who deplore the fact that "industry is the polluter, and it is industry that would receive support for developing pollution treatment technology". That is not the problem: the problem is the difficulties encountered by small and medium-sized enterprises which have an innovative approach in this area, and find themselves in uncertain and difficult markets, for all the reasons mentioned in the present report. The implementation of the (European) principle that "the polluter pays" leads on the one hand to the internalisation of pollution treatment costs by the economy, and on the other hand to the development of "cleaner" technologies and pollution treatment technologies. The "needs" in the area of environmental quality protection lead to the creation of corresponding markets. Only a recognition of this fact can lead institutions to support companies specialising in this sector, and thus to improve our capacity to deal with environmental questions.

- An expansion of the biological portion of these environmental markets is conditioned by a recognition, particularly by the European institutions, of the possible contribution which biotechnology can make in this sector. This is already happening in the EPA in the United States, the Bioremediation Action Committee (BAC) tries to involve the different parties concerned with evaluating the potential of biotechnology for environmental improvement; as a corollary it aims to improve communication between itself and bio-industry.

- Moreover, the existence of clear and transparent policies in the area of biotechnology could reduce uncertainties in these markets.

- In drawing up specifications describing the plants for treating dangerous wastes, it is possible that in certain cases biological procedures may be placed at a disadvantage, in practice, by comparison with other types of procedures (such as incineration, for example). It is undoubtedly necessary that the environmental bio-industry should learn how to make itself known to the authorities in charge of treatment programmes, at all levels.

- Lastly, the best publicity for biological treatment will consist in carrying out and publicising pilot projects which produce convincing results. But these pilot projects are made difficult in the climate which currently prevails in Europe. The measures taken within the EPA (favourable regulations) could usefully be duplicated in Europe.

| Topic IV | Political and public opinion questions |

Questions:

4.1 The non-acceptance of the development of genetic engineering by a portion of public opinion in Europe could lead to the political feasibility of science-based development being called into question. What can European institutions do in this regard? What would be the possible alternatives?

4.2: What measures could be take by European institutions, for example, with a view to improving the understanding of all these questions by the public (in the area of the environment as in the area of biotechnology)?

4.3: How could European institutions more effectively integrate considerations about the environment and socio-economic considerations into the decision-making process?

4.4: What are the points of view in the other regions of the world?

Summary of responses:

- The question of the (democratic) political feasibility of science-based development or the existence of alternatives to this mode of development has not been broached. This may be a new line of research for the Foundation ...

- An improvement of the level of public information and arrangements for communication between science, industry, institutions (administrative and political) and "society" is felt to be necessary and feasible. Projects are being formulated with this in view, particularly within CUBE.

- The representatives of the environmental defence groups and of industry agree that it is necessary to improve the transparency of decision-making and the clarity of policies at European level. From this point of view, the American experience seems different from the European experience: the American agencies seem to carry out dialogue more willingly and more easily with the public, with companies and with pressure-groups.

- The existence, in the Commission document describing European policy on bio-industry, of a reserve clause allowing the Commission to issue an opinion other than one based exclusively on the three usual scientific criteria (quality, efficacy and safety), represents, for the European bio-industry, an added element of uncertainty. According to certain experts, some companies use this to justify their establishment of production facilities or R&D centres in other regions of the world. Others feel that the reasons driving these companies to set up outside Europe must be sought elsewhere.

- The companies interpret this reserve clause, *taken together with the other measures* adopted with regard to genetic engineering, as a possible rejection of this technology by a portion of European society: consequently, they feel that the European market for genetic engineering is partially "closed" to them, in this region of the world.

- Some examples of the financing of information campaigns by European institutions were given.

- In the area of biotechnology, the creation of the BCC (Biotechnology Co-ordination Committee) makes it possible to look to the development of new approaches.

- As regards the development of these questions in other areas of the world, participants heard representatives of the United States and UNIDO (developing countries). Among the latter respondents, concern was focused on the need to establish an international reference framework quickly, so as to harmonise safety measures and release the financial resources which would make it possible for these countries to gain rapid access to new technology. In the United States, the attitude of the public, the authorities and the companies was presented as "more pragmatic" and, perhaps, more open to dialogue and the exchange of views.

Topic V   Regulations

Questions:

5.1   What are the current and future policies of European institutions in the different areas covered by the development of bioremediation?

5.2: How do the European regulations influence the development of this sector?

5.3: Do the regulations currently controlling genetic engineering hamper investments in this sector?

5.4: What is the probable development of the regulations conditioning the environmental market and the biological portion of this market?

Summary of responses:

- The participants formulated recommendations that the evolution of policies should be more favourable to the development of pilot projects in the bioremediation field.

- The EPA (USA) adopts a resolutely positive attitude towards the implementation of such projects.

- The regulations designed to control genetic engineering in the European Community are felt by the companies to be barriers, not only administrative but also "psychological", to the development of innovative technological solutions. Here again, the US Environmental Protection Agency adopts a pragmatic approach: on the one hand it establishes security measures, but on the other hand it has begun a process to evaluate the potential of biotechnology in the environmental sector.

- American participants were of the opinion that "the European Community is being faced with unjustified fears among the public, and a poor image of the technology". They also felt that the European regulations imposed on companies were unjustified obstacles to the process of innovation.

- Nevertheless, we may say that the European regulatory framework (which now exists), currently translated into national law in Member States, could be considered as acceptable by the industry and the scientific world, to the extent that all parties perceive this framework as capable of evolving, for example in the light of experimental results or accumulated experience, in the short term.

- The direction of this evolution (which is foreseen in the Communication of the Commission concerning the competitiveness of European bio-industry) could be as follows:

    1   encouraging a better integration of economic and environmental considerations (analysis of risks and advantages) in decision-making (as envisaged in Article 130R of the Single European Act) and reducing the economic uncertainties caused by regulations which, for lack of clarity or objective criteria, do not allow investors to forecast whether or not their products and procedures will be authorised or not, thus leaving the way open for the possibility of arbitrary decisions which undermine, for example, the healthy rules of competition and openness;

2   providing "one key for each door" (limiting the number of procedures and authorisations required for each type of product launched on the market) - as envisaged in the SEC document (91) 629;

3   ensuring an integration of the experimental scientific basis which becomes available from time to time as trials are carried out, as envisaged in the SEC document (91) 629;

4   envisaging and encouraging a balanced interpretation of these questions by European public opinion;

5   admitting that the risks are of reduced dimensions, that the dangers so far have been of a conjectural kind (trials and their effects/impacts are recorded, for example particularly by the OECD in the BIO-TRACK database);

6   re-evaluating, where necessary - as envisaged in the SEC document (91) 629 - all existing regulations, and the possibility of controlling the uncertainties associated with the use of genetic engineering, in the light of new knowledge.

VI. RECOMMENDATIONS AND SUGGESTIONS TO THE PARTICIPANTS IN THE DEBATE AND THE PARTNERS IN EUROPEAN DECISION-MAKING

(These recommendations have been formulated on the basis of the investigative work presented in the research report, and the discussions which took place during the seminar organised in Dublin.)

VI.1 EUROPEAN INSTITUTIONS

VI.1.1 R&D POLICY (DG XII)

A.   Research in natural and technological sciences

1. The ecology of r-DNA micro-organisms is being studied by research projects within the BRIDGE and BIOTECH programmes. The development of biological techniques for treating pollution is approached within the framework of the STEP programme. It could be useful to intensify the exchanges of information and experience between the experts and the people in charge of the BRIDGE/BIOTECH and STEP programmes, and on the other hand to integrate into future programmes activated in the biotechnology area projects concerned with the applications of genetic engineering to pollution treatment, addressing the aspects of ecology, of safety, of molecular biology and the biological engineering of processes.

2. The new R&D programme in the environmental area includes projects intended to develop better methodologies for assessing the evolution of ecosystems and the impact which economic activities have on them. It would be a good idea for the people in charge of those projects to establish co-operative links with those in charge of the projects in the "bio-security" section of the BRIDGE and BIOTECH programmes.

3. Pilot projects in the "bio-remediation" sector could also be implemented with support from European institutions - and the results of these projects could be communicated to the public.

B. Technology assessment

1. On the same basis as the activities carried out by the Federal agency in charge of environmental matters in America (EPA), a working group could be set up in Europe, to assess the conditions of development for a European "bio-remediation" sector.

2. Based on the project currently implemented by the MONITOR/SAST programme (project no. 4: "Agro-biotechnological innovation"), the departments within the Commission could set up studies to compare the possible contributions of biological (organic), industrial and biotechnological agriculture, in the Community and in other regions of the world, to a possible transition towards "sustainable development" in agriculture.

3. Studies could also be carried out with a view to evaluating how the results of technology assessments are now integrated into decision-making in Europe.

4. A regular assessment of how European societies are taking on board the progress of **knowledge** would also appear desirable. This assessment, which could be based on a regular use of Eurobarometer, could make it possible to improve policies of information and communication on the part of those in charge of scientific and technological development, on the one hand, and socio- economic development, on the other hand.

5. Case studies could be carried out, with a view to identifying the mechanisms by which information produced in scientific terms is "translated" to all levels through mediators or the public, and measures could be taken with a view to limiting the spread of unfounded rumours, unjustified hopes or fears, deriving from all possible sources (scientists themselves, journalists, enterprises, political action groups).

6. To the extent that there seems to be little choice other than science-based development and the progress of knowledge, the problems posed by the acceptance of biotechnology, largely due to communication difficulties, seem to indicate a necessity to provide better information to the public about the true nature of the scientific approach, as it is true that while science is not the only source of truth, it is still often wrongly perceived as having the aim of opposing religion by demystifying life, or else it is seen as a "power" held by people with a "privilege of intelligence" and used for economic purposes in order to widen the gap between the "stronger" and the "weaker". Only a better division of the "power" conferred by knowledge can allow an improvement in the discussion both of decision-making processes leading to progress, and of the effects to which they may lead. An obscurantist condemnation of knowledge-based progress is not the way to make our development process more socially concerned and equitable ...

7. Information to the public relating to experience built up over time, as organisms produced by genetic engineering are used in the environment, and relating to the assessment of administrative methods and procedures for monitoring, is also necessary. This information should make it possible for perceptions to be better adjusted to facts (the existence or non-existence of accidents , for example).

VI.1.2 INDUSTRIAL POLICY

1. The "Panorama of European industry" in 1990 (published by DG III) provides, for the first time, statistical information on the "sector" of pollution treatment in the Community. This shows the growing awareness of the importance of these activities in economic terms. But the assessment and search for new incentives which would help new enterprises, with a high degree of performance and innovation, to be established in these markets is perhaps still to be hoped for. Innovation in this sector is in fact something particularly delicate, especially because priorities in the environmental area are essentially dictated by political - and thus random - considerations.

2. The establishment of a European bio-remediation committee could also be usefully followed up by DG III, within the departments of the Commission.

3. Pilot projects for demonstration purposes in the area of environmental industry could be envisaged by the Commission; their implementation would probably require co-operation between DG XI, DG XII and DG III.

4. It will be important for the Commission, within the framework of its initiatives in favour of SMEs, to pay particular attention to those with activities involved with biotechnology and, in particular, their application to environmental problems.

VI.1.3 ENVIRONMENTAL POLICY (DG XI)

1. The importance for the pollution treatment industry to have clear policies and regulations, and transparent decisions, is beyond doubt. This is necessary both in the case of regulations creating environmental markets, and in the area

of monitoring biotechnology. Confirmation of the existence of possibilities, within defined conditions, of improving the state of the environment through biotechnology, could contribute to an improvement not only in the innovation process in the sector under review, but also in the acceptance of biotechnology in general. A response on this topic from those in charge of DG XI could not be obtained within the context of the present project.

2. An awareness of the economic and social advantages, on the one hand, and the results of bio-security research on the other hand, in the application and development of regulations, could also contribute to an improvement in the political climate within which the European bio-industry is developing.

VI.1.4 BIOTECHNOLOGY CO-ORDINATION COMMITTEE

- The BCC will be able to play a central role by reducing inconsistencies and imbalances which too strong leadership from one or other Directorate General could introduce into the content of future directives. In this way, it would complete the process of inter-departmental consultation which is already in place, but which is sometimes felt, in certain quarters, to contain some gaps.

- Through internal analysis and the commissioning of special studies, the committee will be able to ensure that "forgotten" parameters are taken into account when preparing decisions or initiatives at Community level. Some of these elements with a major influence sometimes seem, at first sight, very far from the subject in question; only an in-depth analysis allows them to be identified and assessed.

- The BCC will be able to encourage constructive dialogue in cases where the approaches of different departments could be so far apart that the consultation process would be reduced to polemics.

- The committee will be able to ensure that cases containing a significant ethical aspect - and only those - will be submitted to the "Ethics Committee".

- In conjunction with CUBE, the committee will be able to promote a process of information and transparency in relation to the public and interest groups.

- It also has the capacity to ensure direct participation, where applicable, of representatives from the "outside world" in its deliberations, whether this involves industrialists, ecologists, researchers or others.

VI.2 ENTERPRISES IN THE ENVIRONMENTAL SECTOR

1. On the basis of the network of participants in the "EUROENVIRON" project in the EUREKA programme, the companies in the environmental sector could set up a "Eur-Eco" association, which could usefully make known the technological developments obtained, and the possibilities offered for improving the state of the environment.

2. The industry will also have to verify the content of information which it disseminated before passing it on to the public, so as to establish and increase its credibility.

VI.3 SCIENTISTS

1. The results of scientific projects in the areas of bio-remediation and the ecology of rDNA ought to be made better known to the public (and better understood). The scientific world can certainly take an active part in the efforts which are necessary in this area.

2. A higher degree of interdisciplinary openness could perhaps have prevented the misunderstandings which can currently be observed between science and society. An interdisciplinary approach supposes an ability to communicate and interpret the results of research projects which can benefit the whole life sciences research community.

VI.4 ECOLOGICAL PRESSURE-GROUPS

1. The questions raised by ecological pressure-groups currently form the subject of research projects financed by the public authorities through European programmes such as BRIDGE/BIOTECH or STEP/EPOCH. There is no reason why participation by these groups in these programmes should be denied - perhaps, on the contrary, it would encourage more openness and an improvement in the dialogue which is necessary for real consideration to be given to their preoccupations.

VI.5 THE EUROPEAN FOUNDATION IN DUBLIN

The question of the democratic viability of our science-based development could be more widely studied by the Foundation in Dublin.

Genetic engineering could be used in this perspective for carrying out case studies.

Annexe I

LIST OF EXPERTS CONTACTED

(*) People who were contacted, but whose views could not be obtained.

BELGIUM

J. Martial, Eurogentec

G. Boeken, Plant Genetics Systems

J. de Brabandere, C. Orfinger, C. Leblicq, L. Molitor
   Science Policy Planning Departments

E.J. Nyns, Catholic University of Louvain

M. Grenson, University of Brussels

J. Verstraete, University of Ghent

N. Nolard, W. Moens, Institut d'Hygiène et d'Epidémiologie

K. Baker, Monsanto

P. Coërs, Solvay Corporation

S. Emmott, Friends of the Earth Coordination

FRANCE

F. Normand, M. Raoux, Elf Aquitaine

J. Manem, M. Bebain Lyonnaise des Eaux

M. le Buanec, Limagrain / GIBIP

J. Theilleux, Rhône-Poulenc

J.P. Lecocq, Transgène

ITALY

M. Buiati, Lega per l'Ambiente

G. Terragni*, G.A.B.

M. Lo Pinto, Agricola 2000

C. Frontali, Istituto Superiore di Sanità

GERMANY

K. Timmis, GBF, Braunschweig
M. De Pelseneer, ARASIN GmbH

UNITED KINGDOM

P. Vernon, Biotreatment
K. Bousfield, NCIMB
M. Lawrence, SERC

EUROPEAN PARLIAMENT

K. Collins
P. Lannoye
L. Bullard*

DEPARTMENTS OF THE EUROPEAN COMMISSION

E. Magnien, I. Economidis, DG XII BRIDGE
M.F. Cantley, O. Diettrich, A. Saint-Rémy, B. Zechendorf, DG XII CUBE
M. Van Delen, DG XII
P. L'Hermite, DG XII STEP
P. Sorup, DG XII STEP
B. Lefèvre, DG XI
E. Salgueiro, DG III
Y. Tachmintzis*, DG XI

EUROPEAN ASSOCIATIONS

J. Murray, ECB

L. Abel, Eureka

C. Taschner, EEB

E. van Landuyt, EFB

B. Ager, CEFIC/SAGB

C. Verschueren, FEDESA

INTERNATIONAL ORGANISATIONS

S. Wald, OECD CPST

U.S.A.

K. Devine, ABTA

J. Doyle, Friends of the Earth

T. Baugh, S. Lingle, E. Milewsky, D. Ogden, M. Segal, EPA

M. Clutter, R. Balstad Miller, NSF

M. Mellon, National Wildlife Federation

M. Steinbock, C. Callaghan, S. Mc Common, USDA

M. Fletcher, Center of Marine Biotechnology

R. Goldburg, Environmental Defence Fund

Annexe II

BIBLIOGRAPHY

(1) Official Journal L117 (8 May 1990)
     90/219/EEC - Council Directive. 90/220/EEC - Council Directive.

(2) U.N. - E.C.E. Bergen Conference - Sustainable development.
     Synthesis paper based on the national reports submitted by ECE member governments - March 1990.

(3) SIIESTA
     Thoughts on the concept of sustainable development: towards a definition (1989).

(4) R. Lichke (IDATE)
     La Juste Communication
     (FAST, 1989)

(5) Public Voice
     A Blueprint for pesticide policy

(6) Biotechnology working group
     Biotechnology, bitter harvest. Herbicide-tolerant crops and the threat to sustainable agriculture (1990)

(7) F. Martin - B. Legru
     Dangerous wastes and the public
     Dublin Foundation

(8) T. Durant
     L'impact de la fonction communication sur les structures sociales
     (1986) FAST

(9) BAP - Progress report 1988 - vol. 4
     Normative research

(10) European Foundation for the Improvement of Living and Working Conditions - ERICA
The Public and Biotechnology - A discussion document (1989)

(11) I. Economidis
European Biosafety Workshop - Berlin (1988)

(12) J.M. Denver - R. Perry - R.M. Sterritt
Dangerous wastes and the public (1988)
Dublin Foundation

(13) International Forum for Biophilosophy: Environment, Health and Industry - The promise of the new biology
Expert meeting (1990)

(14) Dublin Foundation - Working paper series - Social, psychological and economic aspects of contaminated land (1989)

(15) EEC - Modified proposal for a Council directive on the protection of workers against risks connected with exposure to biological agents at work

(16) Pegasus
Biotechnology and the Environment.
Dublin Foundation, 1986.

(17) E.F.B.
Environmental Biotechnology: Future prospects (1982)

(18) CEED meeting - 1985
The Environmental implications and applications of Biotechnology

(19) S. Balajee
Potential role of engineered microbes to detoxify chemical pollutants - a review (1988)

(20) Environmental Biotechnology
TIBTECH - July 1990

(21) B. Dixon
Biotech's effects on diversity
(Bio/technology), June 1990

(22) K. Devine
Environmental factors dictate choice of specific bioremediation methods
Gen. Eng. News, May 1990

(23) S. Lindow
Genetic engineering of bacteria from managed and natural habitat.
Science, vol 244 (1989)

(24) Hazardous waste treatment: potential market for recombinant products.
Gen. Tech. News, Oct. 1988

(25) How Tiny Bugs Eat Pollution
Financial Times, July 30, 1985

(26) World Council of Churches
Biotechnology: its challenges to the churches and the world (1989)

(27) E. Winnacker
A room with a view. The new Biology and the public (1989)

(28) SAGB
Community Policy for Biotechnology: Economic benefits and European competitiveness (1990)

(29) World Bank
The ecological economics of sustainability: making local and short-term goals consistent with global and long-term goals (1990)

(30) BRIDGE (DG XII)
European Laboratories without walls

(31) F. Assouline
Dynamiques agricoles et stratégies de l'industrie phytosanitaire dans les pays en voie de développement
Economie rurale (Dec. 1988)

(32) Safety of Agricultural Biotechnology Seminar, Ghent, 1989

(33) J.L. Pedersen
Technology Policy in Denmark
Biotechnology and Politics
Danish experiences

(34) O. Barre
Public opinion on gene technology in Denmark
1990

(35) SAGB
Community policy for Biotechnology: creation of a Commission task-force and an independent advisory body

(36) J.F. Bunders
Biotechnology for small-scale farmers in developing countries (1990)

(37) SAGB-CEFIC
Community policy for Biotechnology: priorities and actions

(38) Pesticides and food safety
EPA Journal, May/June 1990

(39) National Science Board
National Science Foundation
Science & Engineering indicators (1989)

(40) EEC
Draft proposal for Council regulation on the marketing of genetically modified animals

(41) U.S.D.A.
Draft guidelines for assessing the Environmental impact of research into the environment of organisms with deliberately modified hereditary traits

(42) U.S.D.A.
Agricultural Biotechnology
Introduction to field testing
1990

(43) Biotechnology Field of Dreams
World-watch, Jan 1990

(44) Maryland Sea Grant
The promise of Biotechnology

(45) O.T.A.
New developments in Biotechnology: public perceptions of Biotechnology (1987)

(46) O.T.A.
New developments in Biotechnology: U.S. investments in Biotechnology (1988)

(47) O.T.A.
New developments in Biotechnology:
Field-testing engineered organisms @ genetic and ecological issues (1988)

(48) M. Mellon
National Wildlife Federation
Biotechnology and the Environment (1988)

(49) EPA
Office of Research & Development
Alaskan Oil Spill Bioremediation
Project update (1990)

(50) O.T.A.
New Developments in Biotechnology
Public perceptions of Biotechnology (1987)

(51) National Academy of Sciences
Introduction of recombinant DNA organisms into the Environment (1987)

(51) Chemical firms move to turn waste to profits
Chemical Week, August 1990

(53) The release of genetically engineered organisms: a perspective from the ecological society of America (1989)

(54) Bundestag
Report of the Commission of Enquiry on "Prospects and risks of genetic engineering" (1987)

(55) F.E. Joyce
The Environmental industry in the EEC
FAST 1983

(56) EUREKA
Euroenviron: new opportunities for developing environmental technology

(57) OECD
Biotechnology - Economic effects and other repercussions (1989)

(58) National Research Council
Field testing genetically engineered organisms
Framework for decision (1989)

(59) W. Van Deelen (CEC)
Europeans, science and technology (1990)

Annexe III

ANALYSIS FRAMEWORK

Questions raised with the experts

I. **Biotechnology and the Environment**

1. How are the recent European directives implemented?
2. How are they perceived by scientists, industrialists, pressure groups, governments?
3. What is the meaning of the difference in approaches between the EEC and the USA for regulating biotechnology? How is the rest of the world proceeding?
4. Is there any possible contribution of the new biotechnology (e.g. genetic engineering) for the improvement of the environment?
5. What are the possible bottlenecks in the concerned research fields?
6. What are the conditions for getting biotechnology to ensure a transition to sustainable development?
7. Are there any current developments that are positively detrimental to the environment?
8. Are there any developments that are positively beneficial to the environment?
9. What is the current evaluation of the market potential for environmental biotechnology?
10. Which companies are currently including such products/processes in their development plans/strategies?
11. Are there any adaptations of present policies and regulations which would be necessary for allowing contributions of biotechnology to the improvement of the environment?
12. What are the research priorities in the field?

II. Biotechnology and the Public

1. What are available data on public perception and acceptance of biotechnology?
2. What were the methods used and what are the possible interpretations of the data?
3. How far do we understand the determinants of opinions, attitudes and behaviours of individual lay- people towards science and technology? How is what they feel reflected in the opinion and attitude expressed by pressure groups that are active in the area?
4. How broad is the gap between acceptance and acceptability, as perceived by the "silent majority", pressure groups, politicians, regulators, industrialists and scientists?
5. What is the impact of the present regulatory option chosen by the EEC on public perception of biotechnology? How does it compare to what is being considered in other parts of the world?
6. How does information transfer from science to society?
7. What is the basic position of various religious authorities? How relevant is it to get the opinion of the public?
8. Does the public get a balanced view of necessities, in terms of socio-economic development, and possibilities in terms of science and technology?
9. Is the scientific illiteracy of the public which is observed in most industrialised countries the major component of adverse reactions to biotechnology?
10. What is the importance of other factors - like the lack of trust in the safety of industrial processes after serious accidents (Bhopal, Chernobyl), or the behaviour of some industrialists who have been unable to provide the public with reliable information or else the lack of available fora for people to express their fears and get reasonable answers to their questions?
11. To what extent are the possible contributions of biotechnology to the improvement of the environment widespread known? Is that information supposed to lead to changes in public attitudes?
12. How to get the silent majority to express what is the real perception by "the public"?

Annexe IV

LIST OF THE PRINCIPAL DOCUMENTS
COLLECTED DURING THE STUDY

(1) O. Borre - Public opinion on gene technology in Denmark 1987-1989

(2) National Wildlife Federation - The Gene Exchange Newsletter

(3) USDA - Biotechnology Notes

(4) B.L. Umminger (NSF) - Memorandum

(5) EPA - Summary report on the EPA-Industry meeting on environmental applications of Biotechnology (1990)

(6) ABTA - Get to know ABTA

(7) CCE - DG XII Europeans, science and technology

(8) European Consumers' Bureau - Preparatory note (F. Lamy) -

(9) Federal Register - OSTP - Principles for federal oversight of Biotechnology: planned introduction into the environment of organisms with modified hereditary traits

(10) J. Miller - Risk-based oversight of experiments in the Environment

(11) Counting on science at EPA

(12) W. Verstraeten et al - How can biotechnology solve environmental problems of modern society

(13) Elf Aquitaine - INOPOL Hydrocarbon biodegradation accelerating agent

(14) ARASIN - Bio-catalytical exhaust cleaning

(15) SERC - Clean Technology Programme

(16) K. Collins - On Bio-ethics Committee

(17) Lyonnaise des Eaux applies biotechnology to water quality

(18) M.F. Cantley - Letter to World Council of Churches

(19) Technology Assessment Conference (Milan) FAST
      November 1990

(20) OECD - Group of national experts on safety in Biotechnology (1990)

(21) Agricola 2000 - Biotechnology regulation in Italy

(22) E. Magnien - Biotechnology rhymes in Europe

(23) Italy (PCI) - Proposal for regulating Biotechnology

(24) Italy - GAB: Biotecnologie e Agricoltura

(25) Italy - PCI: Le Biotecnologie avanzate del settore agroalimentare

(26) Biotecnologie e rischio ambientale conference Rome 1990 (programme)

(These documents have been delivered to the Foundation.)

Annexe V

LIST OF THE PARTICIPANTS
IN THE DUBLIN SEMINAR

Belgium

E.J. Nyns	Unité de Génie Biologique
	Université Catholique de Louvain
E. Van Landuyt	European Federation of Biotechnology
P. Schenkelaar	Friends of the Earth
C. Knorr	European Environmental Bureau

Denmark

K.R. Moeller	Danish Parliament
L. Abel	EF-Konsulenterne

France

M. Trouve	Centre de Recherche Lyonnaise des Eaux-Dumez
A. Millet	BIOFUTUR

Germany

D. Brauer	Hoechst AG
D. Dwyer	GBF
H. Fisher	Umweltbundesamt

Portugal

P. Moreno	Amigos da Terra
J.F. Dos santos Oliveira	Universitade Nova de Lisboa

Spain

L. Lemkow	Facultad de Ciencias Politicas y Sociologia
	Universitat Autònoma de Barcelona

United Kingdom

P. Barratt	Biotreatment Ltd
D. Brown	Green Alliance
L. Da Gamma	Bioindustry Association
M. Griffith	Biotechnology Unit
	Laboratory of the Government Chemist
B. Kirsop	Biostrategy Associates Ltd
E. Roberts	ERICA

United States

T. Baugh	Office of the Environmental Engineering and Technology Demonstration
R. Colwell	Maryland Biotechnology Institute
M. Mac Laughlin	US Congress
	Office of Technology Assessment

United Nations

E. Da Silva	UNESCO
I. Tzotzos	UNIDO, International Centre of Genetic Engineering and Biotechnology

Employers

J.F. Thorley	Eli Lilly International Corporation

Trade unions

M. Miller	ETUC

Foundation

C. Purkiss   Director
R. Anderson   Research Manager
C. Galli da Bino   Secretary

Departments of the Commission

M. Cantley   DG XII/F/1 - CUBE
P. Sorup   DG XII/E
I. Economidis   DG XII/F/2
A. Van der Meer   Secretariat General

Annexe VI

LIST OF COMMUNICATIONS TO THE SEMINAR, THE TEXT OF WHICH WAS DELIVERED TO THE FOUNDATION

R. Colwell
Risk assessment in environmental biotechnology

I. Economidis
Transparencies

P. Schenkelaar
The ecological risks of genetically engineered organisms

D. Dwyer
Transparencies

IRRO
Press release

P. Sorup
New R&D programme in the field of environment

D. Brauer
A group of men investigating an elephant

L. Abel
Description of Euroenviron

P. Barratt
Transparencies

T. Baugh
Bioremediation Action Committee

Other studies carried out and published by the Foundation in related areas:

The Impact of Biotechnology on Living and Working Conditions - A selected Bibliography
(ISBN 92-825-7064-9)
Available only in English

This bibliography lists some 600 articles, books, reports and other documents that relate to the impact of biotechnology on living and working conditions. As such it is one of the largest compilations of material of its kind in existence. It updates material located by the European Biotechnology Information Project at the British Library.

The Impact of Biotechnology on Working Conditions
(ISBN 92-825-6767-2)
Available in English and Italian

This report describes the work of a research group in Rome on the impact of biotechnological innovation on levels of employment, on working conditions and on the supply of and demand for trained personnel. The conclusions are that in the short term it is rather unlikely that biotechnology can have a significant impact in creating new jobs, whilst in the medium term there may be significant demand for people with specialist skills. It is possible that in some European countries some companies will find it hard to acquire such people in years to come. Safety regulations relating to biotechnology research and production are reviewed, and it is noted that workplace hazards are a mixture of old and new problems. However, the formation of new business ventures with newly designed facilities and plant, offers an opportunity for advanced safety engineering and progressive policies for the involvement of all employees in such planning.

The international dimension of biotechnology in agriculture
(ISBN 92-8256768-0)
Available in Dutch and English

This study describes the work of a research group in Amsterdam on the impact of biotechnology on agricultural production in the European Community and in less developed countries that export their agricultural products in Europe. Three main areas are surveyed: the market for dairy products, the production of sugar sweetners and the industry that processes starch for use in the food and other industries. In addition, some consideration has been given to the global trade in oilseeds and fats. The principal emphasis is on the effects of product substitution in particular areas, and thus on changes in the volume of production and trade. This leads to important conclusions about likely changes in the structure, location and intensity of agricultural production in Europe, and thus on levels of employment in that sector. The report also endorses the view that whilst biotechnology offers new opportunities for agriculture in developing countries, its utilisation in the industrialised countries is likely to have a serious effect on the export trade on which such developing countries have been forced to depend.

The impact of Biotechnology on the Environment
(ISBN 92-825-7529-2)
Available in English only

This document describes the work of a research group in Copenhagen on the impact of biotechnology on the environment. The highly topical question of the deliberate release of genetically engineered organisms into the environment is discussed, as are the accidental release of organisms from industrial processes, the application of biotechnology in pollution control and the assessment of the environmental impact of new fermentation processes. The considerable value of biotechnological processes in environmental management is emphasized as is the need to develop new test systems and methods of overall process assessment.

The Social Impact of Biotechnology
(ISBN 92-825-7530-6)
Available in English only

This is the work of a research group in Manchester on the possible impact of biotechnology in the field of health care. The economics of innovation in this area are discussed briefly, before a more extended discussion of some of the moral and practical dilemmas that the innovation of highly sophisticated pharmaceutical and medical products pose. These include questions relating to the diagnosis of genetic disease and the ownership of biological material derived from patients' tissues. The report concludes with a review of survey research on attitudes to biotechnology in Europe. The overall intention is to suggest ways of conducting research on one of the first areas to be transformed by biotechnology.

The Impact of Biotechnology on Living and Working Conditions
(ISBN 92-825-7532-2)
Available in English, French, German, Italian, Danish and Spanish

This is the consolidated report covering general historical models of the economic and technological phenomenon of biotechnology, its impact on health care, on agriculture, on work, employment and industrial training, and on the environment. The result is a novel synopsis of a very wide range of material, covering developments within the European Community, that stresses the contingency of future economic and technological development and the need for widespread participation in debates as to how the enormous potential of biotechnology is to be realised in Europe.

The Public and Biotechnology- A Discussion Document
(Ref. No. EF/89/21/EN)
Available free of charge, on request to the Foundation in the following languages:
English, French, German, Italian and Spanish

This paper is presented as a document for discussion. It is derived from an international workshop on "Consumers and Biotechnology" and is written in a style and language intended to reach the widest range of people. As the document points out, everyone should be interested in this subject since developments in biotechnology are likely to affect the daily lives of all of us - our food, medicines and environment. The report considers how the public can be better informed, and the role of the media in this. It reviews specifically how consumer or other public interest organisations may become involved in the debate and the decision making about future applications of biotechnology. It extends an invitation to all to take part in the process of learning and exchange.

Scenarios for Biotechnology in Europe: A Research Agenda
(Ref. No. EF/90/34/EN)
Available in English

This report looks at current trends in biotechnology as applied in the chemical, agricultural and food, health care and pharmaceutical industries. Prospects for further developments are viewed in the context of the changing political, economic and cultural conditions in Europe and elsewhere. The scenario technique is employed to consider different possible futures for biotechnology in relation to both the nature of the production process (mass production or flexible specialisation) and changing consumer demands (related to degree of concern about the environment). The use of scenarios illuminates the ethical and cultural as well as the economic considerations for industrial planning. A set of proposals for feasible research is presented embracing social, ecological and economic questions.

Public Attitudes to Genetic Engineering: Some European perspectives
Available in English, French and Spanish

The attitudes of the general public and of people in diverse interest groups, are influencing the development of biotechnology. As consumers, workers, residents, or opinion formers, the public has expressed a range of views, particularly on genetic engineering. This report draws together results from recent studies in European Community countries to identify key areas of public interest and concern. The results from different research methodologies are reviewed to discuss implications for public information, for participation in the debate on genetic engineering, and for public policy.

European Foundation for the Improvement of Living and Working Conditions

Development of an Environmental Bio-Industry:
European perceptions and prospects

Luxembourg: Office for Official Publications of the European Communities

1993 – 131 pp. – 17 x 23.5 cm

ISBN 92-826-4691-2

Price (excluding VAT) in Luxembourg: ECU 12

Venta y suscripciones • Salg og abonnement • Verkauf und Abonnement • Πωλήσεις και συνδρομές
Sales and subscriptions • Vente et abonnements • Vendita e abbonamenti
Verkoop en abonnementen • Venda e assinaturas

BELGIQUE / BELGIË

**Moniteur belge /
Belgisch Staatsblad**

Rue de Louvain 42 / Leuvenseweg 42
B-1000 Bruxelles / B-1000 Brussel
Tél. (02) 512 00 26
Fax (02) 511 01 84

Autres distributeurs /
Overige verkooppunten

**Librairie européenne /
Europese boekhandel**

Rue de la Loi 244 / Wetstraat 244
B-1040 Bruxelles / B-1040 Brussel
Tél. (02) 231 04 35
Fax (02) 735 08 60

Jean de Lannoy

Avenue du Roi 202 / Koningslaan 202
B-1060 Bruxelles / B-1060 Brussel
Tél. (02) 538 51 69
Télex 63220 UNBOOK B
Fax (02) 538 08 41

Document delivery:

Credoc

Rue de la Montagne 34 / Bergstraat 34
Bte 11 / Bus 11
B-1000 Bruxelles / B-1000 Brussel
Tél. (02) 511 69 41
Fax (02) 513 31 95

DANMARK

J. H. Schultz Information A/S

Herstedvang 10-12
DK-2620 Albertslund
Tlf. 43 63 23 00
Fax (Sales) 43 63 19 69
Fax (Management) 43 63 19 49

DEUTSCHLAND

Bundesanzeiger Verlag

Breite Straße 78-80
Postfach 10 80 06
D-W-5000 Köln 1
Tel. (02 21) 20 29-0
Telex ANZEIGER BONN 8 882 595
Fax 2 02 92 78

GREECE/ΕΛΛΑΔΑ

G.C. Eleftheroudakis SA

International Bookstore
Nikis Street 4
GR-10563 Athens
Tel. (01) 322 63 23
Telex 219410 ELEF
Fax 323 98 21

ESPAÑA

Boletín Oficial del Estado

Trafalgar, 29
E-28071 Madrid
Tel. (91) 538 22 95
Fax (91) 538 23 49

Mundi-Prensa Libros, SA

Castelló, 37
E-28001 Madrid
Tel. (91) 431 33 99 (Libros)
     431 32 22 (Suscripciones)
     435 36 37 (Dirección)
Télex 49370-MPLI-E
Fax (91) 575 39 98

Sucursal:

Librería Internacional AEDOS

Consejo de Ciento, 391
E-08009 Barcelona
Tel. (93) 488 34 92
Fax (93) 487 76 59

**Llibreria de la Generalitat
de Catalunya**

Rambla dels Estudis, 118 (Palau Moja)
E-08002 Barcelona
Tel. (93) 302 68 35
    302 64 62
Fax (93) 302 12 99

FRANCE

**Journal officiel
Service des publications
des Communautés européennes**

26, rue Desaix
F-75727 Paris Cedex 15
Tel. (1) 40 58 75 00
Fax (1) 40 58 77 00

IRELAND

Government Supplies Agency

4-5 Harcourt Road
Dublin 2
Tel. (1) 61 31 11
Fax (1) 78 06 45

ITALIA

Licosa SpA

Via Duca di Calabria, 1/1
Casella postale 552
I-50125 Firenze
Tel. (055) 64 54 15
Fax 64 12 57
Telex 570466 LICOSA I

GRAND-DUCHÉ DE LUXEMBOURG

Messageries du livre

5, rue Raiffeisen
L-2411 Luxembourg
Tél. 40 10 20
Fax 40 10 24 01

NEDERLAND

SDU Overheidsinformatie

Externe Fondsen
Postbus 20014
2500 EA's-Gravenhage
Tel. (070) 37 89 911
Fax (070) 34 75 778

PORTUGAL

Imprensa Nacional

Casa da Moeda, EP
Rua D. Francisco Manuel de Melo, 5
P-1092 Lisboa Codex
Tel. (01) 69 34 14

**Distribuidora de Livros
Bertrand, Ld.ª**

Grupo Bertrand, SA

Rua das Terras dos Vales, 4-A
Apartado 37
P-2700 Amadora Codex
Tel. (01) 49 59 050
Telex 15798 BERDIS
Fax 49 60 255

UNITED KINGDOM

HMSO Books (Agency section)

HMSO Publications Centre
51 Nine Elms Lane
London SW8 5DR
Tel. (071) 873 9090
Fax 873 8463
Telex 29 71 138

ÖSTERREICH

**Manz'sche Verlags-
und Universitätsbuchhandlung**

Kohlmarkt 16
A-1014 Wien
Tel. (0222) 531 61-0
Telex 112 500 BOX A
Fax (0222) 531 61-39

SUOMI/FINLAND

Akateeminen Kirjakauppa

Keskuskatu 1
PO Box 128
SF-00101 Helsinki
Tel. (0) 121 41
Fax (0) 121 44 41

NORGE

Narvesen Info Center

Bertrand Narvesens vei 2
PO Box 6125 Etterstad
N-0602 Oslo 6
Tel. (22) 57 33 00
Telex 79668 NIC N
Fax (22) 68 19 01

SVERIGE

BTJ

Tryck Traktorwägen 13
S-222 60 Lund
Tel. (046) 18 00 00
Fax (046) 18 01 25
           30 79 47

SCHWEIZ / SUISSE / SVIZZERA

OSEC

Stampfenbachstraße 85
CH-8035 Zürich
Tel. (01) 365 54 49
Fax (01) 365 54 11

ČESKÁ REPUBLIKA

NIS ČR

Havelkova 22
130 00 Praha 3
Tel. (2) 235 84 46
Fax (2) 235 97 88

MAGYARORSZÁG

Euro-Info-Service

Club Sziget
Margitsziget
1138 Budapest
Tel./Fax 1 111 60 61
         1 111 62 16

POLSKA

Business Foundation

ul. Krucza 38/42
00-512 Warszawa
Tel. (22) 21 99 93, 628-28 82
International Fax & Phone
(0-39) 12-00-77

ROMÂNIA

Euromedia

65, Strada Dionisie Lupu
70184 Bucuresti
Tel./Fax 0 12 96 46

BĂLGARIJA

Europress Klassica BK Ltd

66, bd Vitosha
1463 Sofia
Tel./Fax 2 52 74 75

RUSSIA

Europe Press

20, Sadovaja-Spasskaja Street
107078 Moscow
Tel. 095 208 28 60
     975 30 09
Fax 095 200 22 04

CYPRUS

**Cyprus Chamber of Commerce and
Industry**

Chamber Building
38 Grivas Dhigenis Ave
3 Deligiorgis Street
PO Box 1455
Nicosia
Tel. (2) 449500/462312
Fax (2) 458630

TÜRKIYE

**Pres Gazete Kitap Dergi
Pazarlama Dağitim Ticaret ve sanayi
AŞ**

Narlibahçe Sokak N. 15
Istanbul-Cağaloğlu
Tel. (1) 520 92 96 - 528 55 66
Fax 520 64 57
Telex 23822 DSVO-TR

ISRAEL

ROY International

PO Box 13056
41 Mishmar Hayarden Street
Tel. Aviv 61130
Tel. 3 496 108
Fax 3 544 60 39

UNITED STATES OF AMERICA/
CANADA

UNIPUB

4611-F Assembly Drive
Lanham, MD 20706-4391
Tel. Toll Free (800) 274 4888
Fax (301) 459 0056

CANADA

Subscriptions only
Uniquement abonnements

Renouf Publishing Co. Ltd

1294 Algoma Road
Ottawa, Ontario K1B 3W8
Tel. (613) 741 43 33
Fax (613) 741 54 39
Telex 0534783

AUSTRALIA

Hunter Publications

58A Gipps Street
Collingwood
Victoria 3066
Tel. (3) 417 5361
Fax (3) 419 7154

JAPAN

Kinokuniya Company Ltd

17-7 Shinjuku 3- Chome
Shinjuku-ku
Tokyo 160-91
Tel. (03) 3439-0121

Journal Department

PO Box 55 Chitose
Tokyo 156
Tel. (03) 3439-0124

SOUTH-EAST ASIA

Legal Library Services Ltd

STK Agency
Robinson Road
PO Box 1817
Singapore 9036

AUTRE PAYS
OTHER COUNTRIES
ANDERE LÄNDER

Office des publications officielles
des Communautés européennes

2, rue Mercier
L-2985 Luxembourg
Tél. 499 28 -1
Télex PUBOF LU 1324 b
Fax 48 85 73/48 68 17

3/93